WALL STREET'S

BEST KEPT
INVESTMENT SECRET

David Vogel

To my wonderful children Jonathan, Evan, Baron, Caitlin, and Ethan

Contents

DEDICATION

In addition to my children, this text is dedicated to Shanee Moret, Shankar Poncelet, Scott A. Travers, Sam Lukes, Laurence Sack, and Robert Steve Ivy. They, during my lifetime, have generously shared their professional knowledge and experiences with me. Cumulatively, their guidance was instrumental as I progressed as a business professional. Like my mentors, I am committed to enhancing the integrity of our business and assisting clients in the realization of their full potential for financial growth. In that sense, it is my pleasure to pass along insights that can help you enhance your financial portfolio.

Whether you are a beginner or intermediate investor, or perhaps an aspiring professional, it is my sincere hope that this book and future volumes will be of assistance to you and your financial well-being.

David A. Vogel

ACKNOWLEDGEMENTS

Credit is due to the following experts and other individuals who have provided valuable assistance in putting together this publication. I want to extend each of these individuals a special *"thank you"*:

Shanee Moret, Shankar Poncelet, Antrea Fergurson, Robert Steve Ivy, Sam Lukes, Patrick Nielsen, Dr. Michael Thorne, Tina Vogel, Randy Thorne, and Scott A. Travers.

Credit is also due because I've drawn upon the finely detailed statistical information provided by the Energy Institute's Statistical Review of World Energy (2023), made accessible through OurWorldInData.org's comprehensive resource on renewable energy. Their credible charts and graphs have enriched the content significantly. I extend my sincerest thanks to them for their contributions, which have allowed me to present the most accurate data clearly and engagingly.

A special thank you to my five beautiful children, who serve as a never-ending source of inspiration. I also extend my deepest gratitude to my two ex-wives, whose paths with mine have significantly shaped the course of my life. Your impact has been profound, leading me to the joys of fatherhood and teaching me invaluable lessons that continue to resonate. For all of that and more, I sincerely thank you.

Note to My Esteemed Readers:

In true C-suite shark style, I've meticulously refined my manuscript, deleting over 27,000 words to present you with the essence of **Wall Street's Best Kept Investment Secret**. Why such a drastic cut? Because the C-suite doesn't just appreciate brevity - it demands it. You're busy leaders who need the distilled wisdom, the crux of strategies, without wading through a sea of words. This version is what I call the *Reader's Digest* version for the busy executive, giving you the potent insights and strategies you need to navigate the investment world efficiently. My commitment is to your time and success. Dive in for a concise, powerful read designed to elevate your investment game sharply and swiftly.

Warmly,

David

david@sunrize.homes

Apex Predators Of The Business World Has A Secret!

enley & Co. points out, there are currently 28,420 centi-millionaires in the World. In a nation (the USA) where there are 23 million millionaires, the benchmark for entering the top 1% is a net worth of $18 million. This staggering figure indicates a clear divide: those who have uncovered the secrets to substantial wealth and those who aspire to.

Throughout the modern era, the most affluent individuals have consistently harnessed government incentives, particularly in the form of grants and forgivable loans (a term I find beautifully oxymoronic). This strategy, often overlooked, operates on the principle of utilizing public resources for private wealth accumulation. These incentives, designed ostensibly for broader economic development, provide a unique leverage point for savvy investors who can navigate the complexities of governmental policies. Furthermore, the utilization of these funds often aligns with government priorities, such as green energy, allowing investors to not only benefit financially but also contribute to socially responsible initiatives. This dual advantage underscores the sophistication required to effectively engage with such opportunities, blending fiscal acumen with an understanding of public policy and societal trends

Such strategies have been instrumental, yet subtly so, in the wealth accumulation of many. As a Business *Shark*, my natural inclination is to reverse-engineer these processes. Through meticulous investigation into the allocation of government funds, specifically regarding their purpose and recipients, I have unearthed a plethora of opportunities. A prime example of this is the current green energy initiatives under Joe Biden's administration, which are channeling hundreds of billions of dollars not only into the coffers of large corporations but also into the hands of astute small business owners as well as the small middle-class millionaire investor.

CEOs & C-Suite members, known for their appreciation of brevity, will find the essence of *Wall Street's Best Kept Investment Secret* distilled into this singular, straightforward concept.: **The most affluent industry titans like for example, Elon Musk, have adeptly leveraged *"free money"* available through government programs, particularly in the green energy sector.**

The strategy of utilizing government grants and forgivable loans significantly contributed to the building of immense wealth of our nation's centi-millionaires and billionaires. It's a simple, yet profoundly impactful secret that has been the cornerstone of success for many at the pinnacle of financial achievement.

The Math is Undeniable Proving Solar Energy Stands as the Premier Investment

In the dynamic world of Wall Street, a new star is rising with unprecedented speed: **Solar Energy.** Powered by the ambitious vision of Joe Biden's administration and fueled by generous government incentives, solar investing is not just an opportunity for financial growth, but a stake in the future of our planet. This book, *Wall Street Best Kept Investment Secret*, unveils the untapped potential of solar investments, guided by the unprecedented incentives under the Inflation Reduction Act. As we delve into the world of solar energy, we'll explore how this sector is not just transforming the energy landscape but also offering a golden opportunity for savvy investors.

At its core, investment is an algorithm, a precise blend of risk and reward, input and outcome. When you infuse this algorithm with the "*free money*" – the governmental incentives spearheaded by Joe Biden's administration – it transforms into not just an opportunity, but the most remarkable investment Wall Street has ever known . . . it all comes down to math!!

Government incentives act as a catalyst, propelling the already compelling solar investment to unprecedented heights. What is happening is a fusion of environmental foresight and financial acumen, driven by an administration committed to renewable energy. This isn't just investing; it's capitalizing on a future sculpted by sustainability and bolstered by governmental support.

In this landscape, solar energy isn't just a sector; it has become the pinnacle of smart investing. It's where the meticulousness of an algorithm meets the unparalleled advantage of governmental backing, creating an investment scenario so potent it's unrivaled in Wall Street's history.

An Investment Move Bobby Axelrod Would Envy!

This investment strategy is so innovative, so brilliantly calculated, that even the legendary Bobby Axelrod would pause and take notice. This is where I, channeling the astute intellect of Taylor Mason, step into the spotlight of Wall Street's grand stage. Embark on a financial journey with me, where mathematical mastery meets market intuition, creating an investment play that's nothing short of extraordinary.

Who's Taylor Mason?

In case you are living under a rock and do not know who Taylor Mason is, They're the epitome of a financial mathematical genius in the cutthroat world of hedge fund trading as portrayed in the hit television show *Billions.*

Taylor, starting as an intern, quickly showcased their extraordinary talent, turning their mathematical prowess into centi-millionaire status.

What Makes Taylor Different?

They're not your typical Wall Street player. Taylor is an oddball, a maverick - someone who doesn't fit the mold but reshapes it. Their unique approach, combining raw intellect with unorthodox strategies, caught the eye of the legendary Bobby Axelrod, a hedge-fund multi-billionaire.

From a nobody with no net worth to a key player in the hedge fund world, Taylor's journey is nothing short of meteoric.

Taylor's success is a testament to the power of math in our lives.

It's everywhere, especially in finance.

The best investment decisions? They're not just about instincts; they're about being a math nerd, about crunching numbers, analyzing trends, and predicting outcomes.

And guess what? I'm a math nerd too! Just like Taylor Mason, I've crunched the numbers and come up with what is the ultimate *Shark* investment. I've poured all this wisdom into this book.

Trust me; the numbers don't lie.

CHAPTER 1

"FREE MONEY?"

When Kevin O'Leary, the celebrated *Shark* and LinkedIn Influencer, speaks of "*free money giveaways*" by the government it's a headline that demands attention.

But what does this mean? Are these incentives, as they relate to commercial solar investments, genuinely "*free money*"?

The term "*free money*" may seem like a misnomer, but in reality, it's a fairly accurate descriptor. When the government provides grants for solar projects, even though taxes are applicable on the grant amount, what remains can indeed be considered free. These funds, earmarked for a specific purpose – solar energy – are not just incentives; they're investments in a sustainable future. For the end user, however, the part of the electricity costs covered by these funds is, effectively, free.

Taking a closer look, some solar energy programs offer more than just grants; with combined government incentives, rebates, and tax credits they promise returns on investment (ROIs) exceeding 100%. It might seem unbelievable, yet it's a reality under the current green energy initiatives.

Diving deeper, it's important to understand that the ROI exceeding 100% specifically pertains to the initial costs of product procurement and construction in designated solar energy programs. This means that with the combined benefits of government incentives, rebates, and other programs, you can recoup the initial investment and then some. Furthermore, once installed, your solar energy system begins producing electricity, essentially converting sunlight into a valuable commodity - electricity, which is, in essence, money. This ongoing production enhances the overall value and returns on your solar investment under the current green energy initiatives.

It's crucial to understand the mechanics of these incentives. They come in various forms, such as the Investment Tax Credit (ITC), and accelerated depreciation benefits, both of which can be stacked with grants and/or forgivable loans.

The cumulation of all benefits sometimes reaches 121% of the cost of the solar project.

Why does the government offer these incentives?

The answer lies in the broader goal of reducing carbon footprints and combating climate change. By making solar energy more accessible, and more affordable the government is not just encouraging a shift towards renewable energy; it's catalyzing a movement towards a greener, more sustainable future.

In light of the political nature of the government funding solar energy debate, it's crucial to refocus the conversation on the tangible impacts of energy choices on our environment and daily lives. Regardless of political affiliations, the consequences of increased carbon emissions and environmental pollution are issues that affect everyone. The real question should not be framed in terms of political ideologies, but rather in terms of sustainability and stewardship of our planet. It's about ensuring clean air, pure water, and a livable environment for future generations. By shifting the focus to these universal concerns, the discussion can move away from divisive political rhetoric and towards constructive, solution-oriented dialogue.

Furthermore, the advancement of solar energy technology presents an opportunity to address environmental concerns in a way that can also spur economic growth and innovation. Investing in solar energy is not just an environmental statement; it's a forward-thinking economic strategy. It opens up new job opportunities, drives technological innovation, and can lead to energy independence. The debate over solar energy and its role in our future should, therefore, be inclusive, encompassing both environmental and economic considerations. By looking at solar energy through this broader lens, we can transcend political divisions and work collectively towards a more sustainable and prosperous future.

For businesses and investors, this presents a unique opportunity. Not only can they contribute to a vital environmental cause, but they also stand to gain financially.

Joe *"Santa Claus"* Biden

Indeed, Virginia, there is a contemporary "Santa Claus" for investors and businesses eager to champion green energy. At this moment, that role is embodied by none other than Joe Biden!

In essence, while the term "*free money*" might initially evoke skepticism, upon closer examination, it becomes apparent that these government incentives are indeed offering a form of financial freedom. They are enabling a shift to renewable energy, which, aside from its environmental benefits, also offers economic gains.

The Wealthiest Individuals Globally Have Capitalized On Grants And Forgivable Loans, Laying The Groundwork For Their Corporate Empires

While a poorer individual might struggle to secure even a few hundred dollars in food stamps from Uncle Sam, the contrast in governmental financial support for the wealthy is stark.

Under the Inflation Reduction Act, for example over 250,000 small businesses are eligible for solar energy systems valued at up to $2 million, entirely funded by Uncle Sam. This disparity highlights how the wealthiest individuals and corporations often have access to significantly larger benefits through grants and forgivable loans. Some of these Green Energy Grants reach astounding amounts, up to $500 million **EACH**, with forgivable loans running in the same ballpark. These substantial financial aids are predominantly accessed by those at the top of the economic ladder, further amplifying their wealth and influence.

The intersection of government policy and corporate benefit, particularly in the context of wealthy individuals and corporations, is a subject that has garnered significant attention and debate. A key example of this is the case of Elon Musk, whose business empire, including Tesla Motors Inc., SolarCity Corp., and SpaceX, has been significantly aided by an estimated $4.9 billion in government support. This support comprises a mix of government contracts, tax benefits, and economic development subsidies. For instance, SpaceX alone received about $20 million in economic development subsidies from Texas for a launch facility and over $5.5 billion in government contracts from NASA and the U.S. Air Force.

Musk's success in obtaining these incentives is notable for both the amount, relative to the size of the companies, and their reliance on them. Musk, who had previously made a substantial sum from eBay Inc.'s $1.5-billion purchase of PayPal, has been able to leverage public subsidies effectively, aiding the rapid growth of his companies.

Another significant case is the U.S. government's bailout of American International Group (AIG) during the financial crisis. The government's overall support for AIG totaled approximately $182 billion, which included nearly $70 billion from the Treasury through the Troubled Asset Relief Program (TARP) and $112 billion from the Federal Reserve Bank of New York. While the bailout was controversial and led to allegations of crony capitalism, the government ultimately realized a positive return of $22.7 billion from its commitment to stabilize AIG during the financial crisis.

These examples illustrate how government subsidies, grants, and bailouts have historically benefitted large corporations and wealthy individuals. While the specifics of each case vary, they collectively paint a picture of significant government support flowing to well-established companies and entrepreneurs.

Attention Millionaires, DecaMillionaires & Centi-Millionaires: Seize Your Share of Green Grants - Money Is Waiting with Your Name On It!

Unlike many grants that cater predominantly to larger entities or the ultra-wealthy, the IRA recognizes the integral role of small businesses in the economy and the green revolution. It provides a comprehensive range of grants, incentives, and tax benefits designed specifically to support both centi-millionaires and middle-class multi-millionaire small business owners.

In the United States, there are 23 million individuals with a net worth of over $1 million so being a millionaire (even a multi-millionaire) is increasingly becoming a marker of the middle to upper-middle class. This demographic, often running or investing in small to medium-sized businesses, is uniquely positioned to leverage these new opportunities. They are at the heart of the economy, driving innovation, and employment, and now, through these grants and incentives, the transition to a more sustainable and green future.

The message of the Inflation Reduction Act to middle-class millionaires is clear: **there is, quite literally, money with your name on it.** This is not just a figurative statement but a literal opportunity. The act opens up avenues for financial support that were previously challenging to access, making it a more level playing field for businesses of varying sizes. These grants and incentives are designed to reduce the financial burden of adopting green technologies, making it an economically viable and attractive proposition for businesses recognized and valued.

So, for every middle-class millionaire out there, the time is ripe to explore how this act can benefit you and how, by stepping forward, you can be part of a larger, global shift towards sustainability and prosperity. *Wall Street's Best Kept Investment Secret* is that the deca-millionaire, even the *"struggling millionaire"* with a small $3 million net worth, can invest like the centi-millionaire sharks when it comes to solar. The playing field is level thanks to Joe Biden's desire to help small businesses.

Let's Journey Forward Together

By delving into the intricacies of this author's favorite solar government programs, you will uncover a wealth of opportunities. These initiatives cover a broad spectrum of sectors, with a notable emphasis on sustainable and green technologies, which are increasingly becoming a cornerstone of governmental funding strategies.

After engaging with the insights and strategies outlined in this book, you should find yourself well-equipped to join the ranks of those who have adeptly navigated this landscape. The goal is not just to inform you about these opportunities but to empower you to actively participate in them. Whether your interest lies in investment opportunities in the burgeoning solar energy sector or leveraging grants for consumer-oriented green initiatives, this book will serve as a comprehensive guide to help you claim your share of these government-funded financial opportunities.

Remember the wealthiest individuals in the USA utilize a power known as "*forgivable loans*" (or grants, a term I sometimes used interchangeably), a beacon of hope and opportunity for companies navigating the tumultuous waters of economic uncertainty.

The following stories unfold with a cast of diverse characters, each a recipient of government money, illustrating the compelling allure and impact of such funding.

In the realm of healthcare, Mariner Health Care Inc., a name synonymous with nursing homes and care facilities, stood at the precipice of receiving a staggering $31 million in maximum SBA funding. This company, acquired by National Senior Care Inc. for $615 million, stretched its caring hands across Southern California and the San Francisco Bay Area, a testament to its expansive reach and the transformative potential of substantial financial support.

Enter Maverick Gaming, a Las Vegas-based behemoth valued at about $1 billion. Owning and operating 26 casinos across three states, the company received upwards of $46 million in loans from the Paycheck Protection Program (PPP). This influx of capital underscored the significant boost that such loans could provide to even the most robust businesses in the entertainment and hospitality sector.

In the specialized world of post-acute care hospitals, Vibra Healthcare emerged as a notable player. Under the leadership of CEO Brad Hollinger, Vibra received at least $13 million in grants and $41 million in loans as part of the CARES Act. These funds bolstered several facilities under Vibra's umbrella, highlighting the critical support these programs could offer to the healthcare industry, even as the company navigated its challenges and past penalties for defrauding Medicare.

The narrative continued with RideNow Powersports Dealers, a chain that experienced nearly tripling its net income from 2019 to 2020. The company received a collective $19 million in PPP loans, fully forgiven, illustrating the substantial relief and financial benefit these loans could provide. Subsequently, RideNow was acquired by RumbleOn, marking a new chapter in its journey.

Acme United Corporation, known for its first-aid supplies, saw a 15% increase in sales in 2020. It received a fully forgiven PPP loan of $3.5 million, demonstrating that even industries experiencing growth could significantly benefit from these loans.

Meanwhile, Conifer Holdings, an insurance company, navigated the pandemic's unpredictable waters with a $2.7 million PPP loan. Despite revenue growth due to lower claims during pandemic shutdowns, the loan was fully forgiven, underscoring the breadth of businesses that these programs supported.

Ammo Inc., the ammunition manufacturer, and Prosper, a venture-capital-backed lending marketplace, both utilized PPP loans to navigate their unique financial landscapes. While Ammo Inc. retained its $1 million loan after expenses, Prosper, with significant cash reserves, received an $8.4 million PPP loan, with its forgiveness request still pending.

As the narrative shifted to technology and innovation, Luminar Technologies, an autonomous driving technology startup, made a strategic move by returning its $7.8 million PPP loan before its Nasdaq debut. Similarly, Velodyne Lidar, after receiving $10 million in government money and going public, saw its loan forgiven, reflecting the complex decisions companies faced in balancing public perception and financial strategy.

Proterra, a battery-powered bus maker, and Dream Finders Homes, a homebuilder experiencing significant earnings growth, both received and decided to keep substantial PPP loans. These decisions, driven by the desire to maintain full workforces and capitalize on growth opportunities, painted a picture of the strategic considerations that went into accepting and utilizing government-funded programs.

These stories, each unique yet interconnected, underscore the significant benefits that well-established and financially robust companies and individuals have reaped from government-funded programs. They serve as a motivation for action, a call to understand and utilize the available resources to navigate the business landscape strategically. As we turn the page on this narrative, let the lessons and insights gleaned inspire a new chapter of informed decision-making and strategic planning for the future.

CHAPTER 2

The Solar Energy Surge

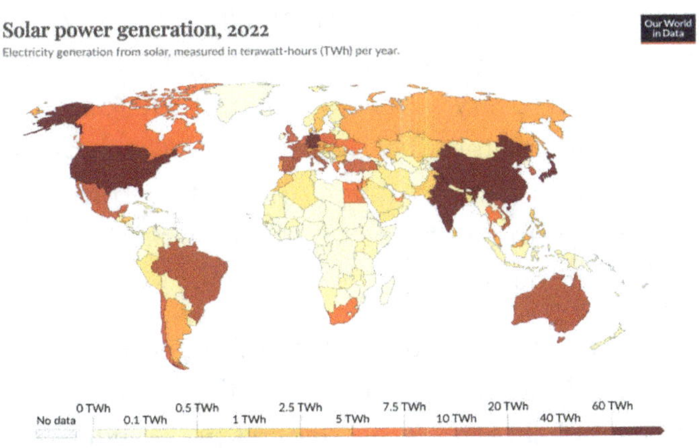

Data source: Ember's Yearly Electricity Data; Ember's European Electricity Review; Energy Institute Statistical Review of World Energy
OurWorldInData.org/renewable-energy | CC BY

The solar industry, once a fringe player in the vast arena of energy production, has rapidly ascended to the forefront of the global economic stage. This meteoric rise is attributed to a perfect storm of technological advancements, environmental urgency, and now, crucially, the proactive approach of the Biden administration. The Inflation Reduction Act, a landmark piece of legislation, has been a game-changer, providing substantial subsidies and tax credits that have supercharged the solar sector. This strategic move signals a significant shift in policy focus towards sustainable energy solutions, making solar investments an enticing prospect for Wall Street Investors.

But why solar?

The answer lies in the unique nature of this energy source. Solar power, unlike fossil fuels, is abundant, sustainable, and environmentally friendly. A staggering 1.8 x 1017 joules of energy from the Sun hits the Earth every second. Averaged over an entire year, approximately 342 watts of solar energy fall upon every square meter of Earth. This is a tremendous amount of energy — **44 quadrillion watts of power to be exact.**

In layman's terms — The sun showers the Earth with enough energy every hour to meet the world's power needs for a full year. Harnessing this power effectively and efficiently has been the quest of scientists and engineers for decades. Now, with the advent of cutting-edge photovoltaic technology, this quest is turning into a lucrative reality.

The impact of solar energy on the global economy and environment is profound. By transitioning from traditional fossil fuels to solar power, we are not only reducing our carbon footprint but also paving the way for a more sustainable and stable economic future. The solar industry has created millions of jobs worldwide, spurred economic growth in numerous sectors, and is playing a pivotal role in the fight against climate change. This is not just an environmental movement; it is an economic revolution.

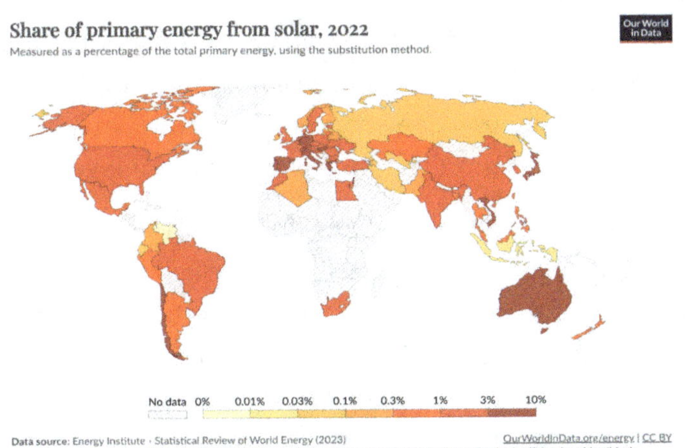

Investors are quickly recognizing the potential of solar energy. The sector has seen a remarkable influx of capital, with solar stocks outperforming many traditional energy stocks. Major corporations and small businesses alike are investing in solar projects, not only to reduce their environmental impact but also to benefit from the financial incentives offered by governments worldwide. This surge in solar investments is a testament to the growing confidence in the renewable energy sector and its potential for long-term profitability.

The Inflation Reduction Act is particularly noteworthy for its comprehensive approach to promoting solar energy. The act provides incentives not only for large-scale solar projects but also for individual homeowners and small businesses. These incentives include tax credits for installing solar panels, subsidies/grants for solar manufacturing, and funding for research and development in solar technology. This broad-based approach is designed to accelerate the adoption of solar energy across the economic spectrum, making it accessible and attractive to a wide range of investors.

This book delves deep into the intricacies of solar investing in the Biden era. I will explore the factors driving the growth of the solar market, the specific incentives provided under the Inflation Reduction Act, and how investors can capitalize on this burgeoning sector. Through expert insights, case studies, and market analysis, I aim to provide a comprehensive guide for anyone looking to invest in one of the most promising and impactful sectors of our time.

As we embark on this journey, it is important to recognize that investing in solar energy is more than just a financial decision. It is a commitment to a cleaner, more sustainable future. The solar industry is at a tipping point, with the potential to transform not only our energy landscape but also our economic and environmental future.

A Brief History Of Solar

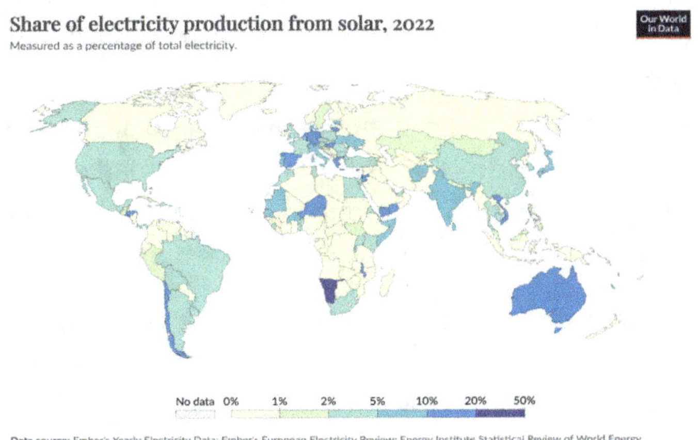

Data source: Ember's Yearly Electricity Data; Ember's European Electricity Review; Energy Institute Statistical Review of World Energy
OurWorldInData.org/energy | CC BY

In recent years, the solar energy sector has emerged as one of the most dynamic and rapidly evolving segments of the global energy market. This transformation is driven by a confluence of technological advancements, regulatory shifts, and a growing awareness of the urgency to transition to renewable energy sources. As we stand at the cusp of a new era in energy production, it's crucial to understand the landscape of solar energy — its past, present, and the promising future it holds.

The roots of solar energy are not as recent as one might think. The concept of harnessing the sun's power dates back to ancient civilizations, which revered the sun and recognized its capacity to provide warmth and light. However, the journey from rudimentary sun worship to today's sophisticated photovoltaic cells spans centuries of scientific discovery and technological innovation.

The modern solar energy movement gained significant momentum in the latter half of the 20th century. With the oil crises of the 1970s, there was a newfound interest in developing alternative energy sources, leading to the first major wave of solar energy research and development. This period marked the birth of the photovoltaic effect in silicon, laying the groundwork for the first solar panels.

Fast forward to the 21st century, and the landscape of solar energy has transformed dramatically. Advancements in photovoltaic technology have drastically increased the efficiency and reduced the cost of solar panels. Economies of scale, coupled with significant investments in research and development, have made solar energy more accessible and affordable than ever before.

Today, solar energy is not just a niche player in the energy market; it's a frontrunner in the renewable energy revolution. Nations around the world are rapidly scaling up their solar energy capacities, driven by the dual incentives of environmental sustainability and economic pragmatism. Solar farms, sprawling fields of photovoltaic cells, have become a common sight in many parts of the world, symbolizing the shift towards a cleaner, greener future.

However, the journey of solar energy is not without its challenges. Issues such as energy storage, grid integration, and the environmental impact of solar panel production are critical topics that need to be addressed to ensure the sustainable growth of the solar sector. Additionally, the solar energy market is intricately linked with global politics and economic policies, making it susceptible to fluctuations and shifts in the geopolitical landscape.

As we explore the current state of solar energy, it's important to recognize that we are witnessing a pivotal moment in the history of energy production. Solar energy, once a mere dream in the eyes of visionaries, is now a tangible, vital part of our global energy portfolio.

The historical context of solar energy is a fascinating journey that stretches back centuries, long before it became a buzzword on Wall Street or a cornerstone of environmental policy. So let's delve into the evolution of solar energy, tracing its origins from ancient times to its current status as a key player in the global energy market.

The Dawn of Solar Understanding

The story of solar energy begins in ancient civilizations, where the Sun was revered not only as a deity but also recognized for its vital role in life. Ancient Greeks, Egyptians, and Romans harnessed solar power using passive solar design in architecture, which utilized the Sun's heat and light efficiently. The famous Roman bathhouses, for instance, were designed to maximize sunlight for heating.

However, it wasn't until the 7th century B.C. that the use of solar energy for practical purposes was recorded. Ancient people used magnifying glasses to concentrate the sun's rays to start fires for cooking and heating. This rudimentary understanding laid the foundation for future exploration of the Sun's potential.

The Scientific Revolution and Solar Power

The scientific revolution in the 17th and 18th centuries set the stage for significant advancements in understanding solar power. Scientists like Isaac Newton began studying sunlight and optics, gradually unraveling the mysteries of light and energy.

In 1767, Swiss scientist Horace-Bénédict de Saussure created the first solar oven, an insulated box covered with three layers of glass to trap the Sun's heat. This invention demonstrated the practical use of solar energy for heating and is considered a significant milestone in solar technology.

The Birth of Photovoltaics

The true birth of modern solar energy can be traced to the discovery of the photovoltaic effect. In 1839, French physicist Edmond Becquerel discovered that certain materials produced small amounts of electric current when exposed to light. This groundbreaking discovery laid the foundation for photovoltaic technology, although it would be decades before the invention of the first solar cell.

The late 19th and early 20th centuries saw a flurry of patents and theoretical work related to solar energy. Inventors like Charles Fritts created the first solar cells made from selenium wafers. However, these early solar cells were highly inefficient and not practical for widespread use.

The Mid-20th Century: Turning Point in Solar Energy

The mid-20th century marked a turning point in the history of solar energy. The space race between the United States and the Soviet Union accelerated solar technology development, as both superpowers sought reliable power sources for their space equipment. In 1958, the Vanguard I satellite was powered by solar cells, demonstrating the practicality of solar power in space applications.

This era also witnessed significant advancements in the efficiency of solar cells. In 1954, Bell Labs in the United States invented the first practical silicon solar cell. This cell was capable of converting enough solar energy into electricity to power small electrical devices, a breakthrough in solar technology.

The Oil Crisis and the Solar Boom

The oil crisis of the 1970s was a critical moment for solar energy. As oil prices skyrocketed and concerns about fossil fuel supplies grew, the world turned its attention to alternative energy sources, including solar power. This period saw increased government and private investment in solar research and development.

In the following decades, advancements in solar technology, along with policy support, led to a gradual decrease in the cost of solar panels. The energy crisis had effectively kicked off a solar boom, with countries around the world beginning to invest heavily in solar energy as part of their energy portfolios.

The 21st Century: Solar Energy Comes of Age

The 21st century has seen solar energy come of age. Technological advancements have made solar panels more efficient, durable, and affordable, leading to a dramatic increase in solar installations worldwide. Solar power is no longer seen as a niche or experimental energy source but a viable alternative to traditional fossil fuels.

Governments around the world have recognized the potential of solar energy in reducing carbon emissions and combating climate change. This has led to policies and incentives to promote solar energy use, including feed-in tariffs, tax credits, and renewable energy targets. The solar industry has become a significant job creator and a driver of economic growth.

The Future of Solar Energy

As we look to the future, solar energy is poised to play an even more significant role in the global energy mix. Innovations such as solar tiles, floating solar farms, and advances in energy storage technology are pushing the boundaries of what's possible with solar energy.

The historical context of solar energy is a testament to human ingenuity and persistence. From the early recognition of the Sun's potential to modern photovoltaic technology, solar energy has evolved into a key solution for our energy needs and environmental challenges. As this technology continues to advance and become more integrated into our daily lives, the story of solar energy remains one of the most exciting chapters in the ongoing quest for sustainable and clean energy sources.

These advancements collectively paint a picture of a solar energy landscape in rapid transformation, driven by both technological innovation and shifting economic and policy landscapes. The future of solar energy, with its increasing efficiency, cost-effectiveness, and integration into broader energy systems, holds significant promise for a sustainable and economically viable energy future.

Global warming: monthly temperature anomaly

The combined land-surface air and sea-surface water temperature anomaly is given as the deviation from the 1951–1980 mean.

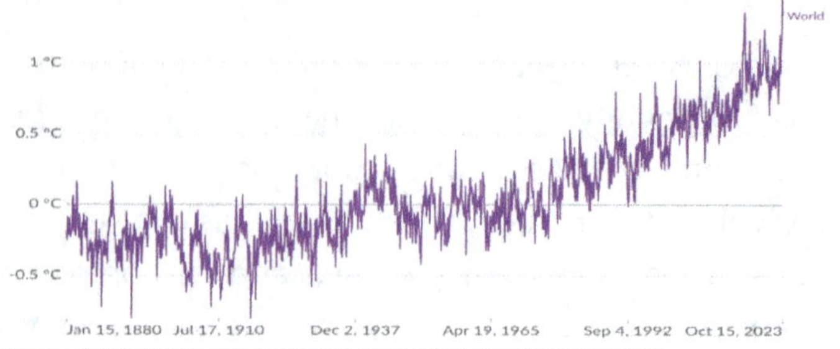

Data source: National Aeronautics and Space Administration (NASA), Goddard Institute for Space Studies (GISS)
CC BY

CHAPTER 3

SOLAR TAKES A QUANTUM LEAP

The Inflation Reduction Act (IRA) is nothing short of a kiss from the Mouth of God for the solar industry, representing the most generous government giveaway in green energy history.

As a savvy investor or businessperson, when you grasp the staggering extent of government subsidies for eco-friendly transitions, it's a moment of pure exhilaration. This legislation is a feast for the apex predators of the investment world, offering tantalizing opportunities at every level.

For the centi-millionaire investor, the IRA lays out a golden path to own a $100 million solar farm, and after calculating the government benefits, you will get back up to 111% of your investment in forgivable loans, tax credits, and other subsidies. Not to mention, you now own a $100 million asset that Uncle Sam paid for. And, that asset produces electricity every day there is sunlight—electricity is a fungible asset that you can convert to Green United States Dollars.

And, as I pointed out, the IRA is not just the realm of the ultra-wealthy; even smaller investors and business owners (middle-class-millionaires to deca-millionaire) can capture their piece of the sun with a $2 million solar energy system for their business (or to own as an investment) paid for by government funding.

This is an unprecedented chance to invest in a sustainable future, with the government effectively rolling out the red carpet for green investments.

Will These Wonderful Benefits Last?

The politicization of solar energy and its associated policies is a significant aspect of the current energy and environmental debate. Generally speaking, the Republican Party has historically expressed skepticism about using government money to subsidize solar energy and other renewable sources, often citing concerns about their cost, efficiency, and impact on traditional energy industries. On the other hand, the Democratic Party typically champions the use of renewable energy sources, including solar, as part of a broader strategy to combat climate change and move towards a more sustainable future.

In the context of the IRA, which was championed by President Joe Biden and his administration, there has been a clear partisan divide. The GOP has criticized the IRA for what they perceive as its excessive spending and potential economic impact. They argue that it represents an overreach of government intervention and expresses concerns about the long-term economic implications, especially about traditional energy sectors.

However, for shrewd investors and environmentally conscious individuals, the political rhetoric surrounding the IRA and solar energy might be less relevant compared to the practical benefits it offers. The IRA, with its provisions for renewable energy investments, opens up opportunities for individuals and businesses to invest in solar energy. This can be viewed as a chance to capitalize on government incentives for adopting renewable energy sources.

From an investor's perspective, these incentives can be seen as a return on the taxes paid to the government. In other words, by taking advantage of the provisions in the IRA, investors are essentially harnessing the benefits of their contributions (through taxes) to the country's infrastructure and environmental policies. This viewpoint reframes the act of investing in solar energy not just as an environmentally responsible decision, but also as a financially prudent one, irrespective of the broader political debate.

In summary, while the debate around solar energy and the IRA is deeply entrenched in political ideologies, for individual investors and environmentally conscious citizens, these policies present practical opportunities. They offer a chance to engage with and benefit from renewable energy investments, thereby contributing to both personal financial growth and the broader goal of sustainable environmental practices.

As the GOP voices concern about the IRA's boldness, saying Joe Biden is *"mad,"* the response from shark investors should be resounding . . . . .
. . . *"Who cares?"*

You've diligently paid your taxes, and now it's your turn to harness what the government offers. Think of this as reaping the returns on your investment (taxes) in the United States of America.

<u>Key Takeaway</u>: For those with investment capacities ranging from $1 Million to as much as $100 Million, the solar energy sector is ripe with attractive incentives. The Inflation Reduction Act significantly enhances this appeal. Moreover, business owners with considerable electricity demands will find President Biden's initiatives towards eco-friendly solutions particularly enticing due to the substantial financial incentives for transitioning. Whether you're an investor or a business proprietor, embracing the green energy movement is a decision that's not only ecologically prudent but also financially savvy.

A Short History of the Inflation Reduction Act of 2022

One of the pivotal actions under Biden's administration has been the signing of the Inflation Reduction Act of 2022. This landmark legislation earmarks a whopping $370 billion for climate and energy spending, with a significant portion dedicated to supporting renewable energy and climate resilience. It mandates a nationwide reduction of carbon emissions by 40% by 2030. The Act also includes provisions to facilitate energy savings for Americans, such as a 30% tax credit for families installing solar on their roofs (the tax credits shoot up to as much as 50% for businesses). Moreover, the IRA emphasizes the development and installation of 950 million solar panels by 2030, alongside other renewable energy infrastructures like wind turbines and grid-scale battery plants.

In addition to financial investment, the Biden Administration has announced several initiatives to advance U.S. solar manufacturing and lower energy costs. For instance, $56 million, including $10 million from the Bipartisan Infrastructure Law, has been allocated to spur innovation in solar manufacturing and recycling. This funding is aimed at making clean energy more affordable and reliable, creating good-paying jobs, and enhancing U.S. economic growth and competitiveness. The focus is also on developing domestic solar manufacturing, reducing reliance on foreign supply chains, and supporting newer technologies like perovskite solar cells.

Biden's executive order on Federal Sustainability also plays a critical role. This order intends to transform the federal government's infrastructure towards zero-emission vehicles and buildings powered by carbon-pollution-free electricity. The order sets ambitious goals, such as achieving 100% carbon pollution-free electricity use by 2030 and modernizing federal buildings to reach net-zero emissions by 2045.

The administration has also launched new solar initiatives to lower electricity bills and create clean energy jobs. For example, the Community Solar Subscription Platform is designed to connect community solar projects with households participating in government-run assistance programs, expected to lead to significant electricity bill savings in multiple states.

Overall, President Biden's policies and investments represent a comprehensive approach to bolstering the solar energy sector. These initiatives not only aim to enhance the United States energy independence and address climate change but also focus on creating jobs and fostering equitable access to clean energy.

Overall Impact

In summary, the policies introduced by the Biden administration represent a comprehensive approach to advancing solar energy in the United States. These policies are not only instrumental in accelerating the transition to renewable energy but also crucial in addressing climate change, promoting domestic energy security, and ensuring equitable access to clean energy technologies.

The Inflation Reduction Act (IRA) has become a significant catalyst for change in various sectors of the economy, but it holds a particularly special place in the heart of the solar industry. In an era where sustainable energy solutions are paramount, the solar industry has been granted substantial benefits through the IRA, specifically in the form of grants and forgivable loans. These incentives have not only fueled innovation but have also propelled the industry toward a brighter, cleaner future.

At the heart of the matter are the 2,554 grants that the Federal Government has authorized, some potentially worth up to a staggering $500 million for an individual grant. This represents a monumental opportunity for solar businesses and entrepreneurs to make substantial strides in renewable energy projects. The significance of these grants cannot be overstated, as they provide a lifeline for those seeking to expand solar initiatives and push the boundaries of what's possible in sustainable energy generation.

One of the most notable aspects of these grants is their scalability. Solar projects, whether on a local or national scale, require substantial investments in infrastructure, technology, and human resources. The grants authorized by the IRA offer the financial backing necessary to turn ambitious plans into actionable projects. This scalability allows solar companies to dream big, pushing the boundaries of innovation while reducing their carbon footprint.

Furthermore, the forgivable loans offered under the IRA are a testament to the government's commitment to fostering the growth of the solar industry. These loans, if utilized strategically, can provide solar businesses with the financial freedom needed to explore groundbreaking technologies, expand operations, and create more jobs. The forgivable nature of these loans reflects the government's confidence in the industry's potential to drive economic growth and environmental sustainability.

The impact of IRA on the solar industry extends beyond the financial benefits. It serves as a beacon of hope for a world grappling with the effects of climate change. The grants and forgivable loans incentivize solar businesses to explore new frontiers in renewable energy, pushing the boundaries of what can be achieved. In an era where environmental consciousness is at the forefront, the IRA offers the support needed to make a difference.

The solar industry has always been at the forefront of technological advancement, constantly pushing the envelope to harness the power of the sun more efficiently. The grants and forgivable loans authorized by the IRA provide a cushion of financial support that enables solar companies to take calculated risks and explore uncharted territories. This innovation doesn't just benefit the industry; it benefits society as a whole by driving down the cost of renewable energy and making it more accessible to the masses.

Moreover, the Inflation Reduction Act aligns with the global shift towards sustainable energy sources. As nations around the world strive to reduce their carbon emissions, the solar industry stands as a key player in this transformation. IRA's support amplifies the industry's efforts to transition from fossil fuels to cleaner, more sustainable alternatives, ultimately contributing to a greener planet for future generations.

In conclusion, the Inflation Reduction Act has become a game-changer for the solar industry, offering a lifeline of grants and forgivable loans that empower businesses to innovate, expand, and lead the charge in sustainable energy solutions. Some grants to go Green with Solar are as little as $50,000, others are as much as $500 million each, and the financial backing is substantial. IRA's support not only drives the solar industry forward but also propels us toward a cleaner, more sustainable future.

Under the leadership of President Joe Biden, the United States has embarked on a transformative journey toward a solar-powered future. This vision, deeply rooted in the administration's commitment to combating climate change and fostering sustainable growth, aims to reshape America's energy landscape by significantly expanding the role of solar energy.

CHAPTER 4

Decoding The Solar Investment Opportunity

In recent years, the solar energy sector has emerged as a lucrative and sustainable investment opportunity. Driven by technological advancements, favorable policies, and a growing global commitment to renewable energy, solar investments offer a unique blend of financial returns and environmental stewardship. In this analysis, we decode the various aspects of investing in solar energy, highlighting its potential as a wise investment choice for the future.

Growth Trajectory and Market Potential

The solar energy market is witnessing a significant upswing, largely due to the decreasing costs of solar technology and the enhanced efficiency of solar panels. This trend has made solar power increasingly competitive with traditional energy sources. Additionally, a heightened awareness of environmental issues is fueling a global surge in demand for solar energy.

Countries worldwide are amplifying this momentum, setting ambitious renewable energy targets and incentivizing solar energy through various policies.

This global push towards decarbonization, coupled with corporate commitments to sustainability, is opening new growth avenues in the solar sector.

Investors have diverse options to engage in this burgeoning market. Direct investment in solar projects, like owning solar farms or rooftop installations, offers a hands-on approach. For those preferring less direct involvement, solar funds or bonds provide diversified, less capital-intensive opportunities. The solar market also includes stocks of companies involved in solar panel manufacturing or solar farm development. While these stocks can be volatile, they present the potential for substantial returns. Additionally, Real Estate Investment Trusts (REITs) focusing on renewable energy infrastructure offer a stable investment avenue in the renewable sector.

However, like any investment, solar energy involves risks such as regulatory changes, technological obsolescence, and market volatility. The intermittent nature of solar power also poses challenges for energy storage and grid integration. Despite these challenges, advancements in energy storage and supportive government policies are improving solar energy's reliability and reducing investment risks.

Investing in solar energy aligns with both financial goals and environmental responsibility. It contributes to carbon emission reduction, combats climate change, generates jobs, and stimulates economic growth, especially in regions transitioning from fossil fuels. The future of solar energy investment appears promising, with ongoing global commitment to renewable energy and technological advancements enhancing solar efficiency and accessibility. This market presents a unique opportunity for investors to contribute to a sustainable future while potentially reaping significant financial rewards.

The solar market, while promising, faces challenges such as the intermittent nature of solar energy impacting storage and grid stability, potential regulatory changes affecting market dynamics, and technological disruptions that could make current solutions obsolete. However, the future is optimistic, with rising global energy demands, a shift towards decarbonization, advancements in storage technology, and opportunities in emerging markets. Investment avenues include direct solar project investments, solar stocks and ETFs, and green bonds. Despite challenges, the sector's robust potential, driven by technological innovations, policy support, and declining costs, positions it as a sustainable and promising investment field in the evolving clean energy landscape.

The Deloitte Study

The Deloitte study on the U.S. solar market, conducted in 2023, provides a comprehensive look at the current state and future outlook of the solar energy sector. The study is backed by Deloitte's extensive experience in energy market analysis, making its findings particularly credible and insightful.

Deloitte's 2023 Renewable Energy Industry Outlook highlighted several key trends and challenges facing the solar industry. Despite some headwinds like supply chain disruptions and rising costs (costs are way down for panels and most solar products), the industry is set to experience robust growth, driven by strong demand and the incentives provided by the Inflation Reduction Act (IRA).

The study also emphasizes the importance of domestic manufacturing in easing supply chain issues, the potential of decarbonized fuel like green hydrogen, and the need for cybersecurity measures as the industry grows. It notes the increasing focus on energy equity, with renewable providers expanding into low-income communities, and the evolving role of offshore wind in the energy mix.

In terms of numbers, Deloitte's 2024 industry outlook, as reported by *PV MAGAZINE* USA, states that in the first eight months of 2023, utility-scale solar capacity additions in the U.S. reached almost 9 GW, outpacing other generation sources and growing 36% over the same period in 2022. The U.S. Energy Information Administration expects utility-scale solar to more than double compared to 2022 by the end of the year. This growth is attributed to the combined demand for decarbonization and federal investments like the IRA and the Infrastructure Investment and Jobs Act (IIJA).

Furthermore, the report mentions significant investment trends, such as the $227 billion invested in utility-scale solar, storage, wind, and hydrogen, spurred by the IRA and IIJA, with $100 billion of these investments already materialized. It also highlights the reshoring of the supply chain, with $91 billion in investments announced and $9.6 billion in 38 solar projects, which could more than triple the year's solar module capacity by 2024.

These insights from Deloitte's study underscore the dynamic and rapidly evolving nature of the U.S. solar market, pointing towards a future where solar energy plays a central role in the country's energy mix.

SOLAR FOR INVESTORS: SEIZING THE SEITS AND SOLAR FARM OPPORTUNITY

Brace yourself for an exhilarating revelation in solar investments, an exciting avenue that's rapidly gaining momentum - the phenomenal fusion of Solar Energy Investment Trusts (SEITs) and solar farms. Lesser-known but rising stars in the investment galaxy, SEITs are sparking a revolution in the solar industry, promising not just radiant returns but also a brighter future for our planet. Get ready to ride this wave of solar supremacy and see your investments shine!

SEITs are essentially investment vehicles that own and operate commercial and utility-scale solar assets, much like how Real Estate Investment Trusts (REITs) function in the property market. These SEITs could include large-scale solar farms, which are massive installations of solar panels generating substantial amounts of electricity.

With the current U.S. administration heavily favoring green energy policies, the incentives for harnessing solar power have never been more enticing. Furthermore, we're now observing a surge in corporations seeking to purchase solar leases, injecting yet another avenue for profitability into the sector.

Remarkably, solar power's investment allure doesn't just stop at the high return on investment and the profit boost from selling solar leases. Solar Farms convert seemingly idle land into a revenue-generating, eco-friendly powerhouse. The environmental benefits to Planet Earth are substantive.

The federal government is throwing its weight behind solar farms, providing grants, large forgivable loans, and incentives to stimulate growth in this sector. These incentives make solar farms even more attractive as an investment. As they generate electricity, the income from power purchase agreements (PPAs) and other contracts is collected and distributed to investors, thus providing an appealing and sustainable investment opportunity.

As an investor, participating in a SEIT gives you the chance to diversify your portfolio with a slice of the clean energy sector. You gain access to the booming solar industry while enjoying potential steady returns.

SEITS And Investment Funds Take Advantage of IRA Benefits

The U.S. Department of Energy coupled with the Inflation Reduction Act will fund billions in grants for solar farms and solar energy projects. This will drive down the cost of solar and accelerate its deployment. When you factor in government grants and subsidies the math makes sense to any potential investor who wants to build a solar farm for fun and profit!

FYI, the government is not the only source of significant funding. Private funding for solar projects has been growing steadily. In 2019, Goldman Sachs committed $150 billion to finance and invest in clean energy, while Bank of America pledged $300 billion by 2030. These massive financial commitments underline the confidence that institutional investors have in the growth and profitability of the solar industry.

The $64,000 Question?

Why aren't all fund managers and investor 'sharks' seizing these lucrative government incentives? The primary barriers are awareness and comprehension. A significant number of investors and business owners are either unaware of these financial opportunities or lack the requisite knowledge to utilize them effectively. This is especially prevalent in complex sectors like solar energy, where understanding the intricacies of both the technology and the government incentives requires a specialized skill set that many may not possess.

That's where the role of a premier consultant becomes invaluable. They don't just offer advice; they provide a roadmap, leading companies through the process of application, implementation, and optimization of government funds. They ensure that businesses not only secure the funding they need but also utilize it in the most effective manner possible, aligning with both business objectives and broader environmental goals.

As part of this advisory, I always recommend hiring a member of the Grant Professionals Association (GPA). The GPA is an organization committed to advancing the grants profession through education, professional development, and ethical practices. Members of the GPA adhere to a strict code of ethics and standards of practice, ensuring that they provide the highest quality of service, maintain confidentiality, and act in the best interest of their clients. Their expertise is not just in securing funds but in understanding the full scope of grant opportunities and requirements. As a member myself, I can attest to the value and integrity that these professionals bring to the table.

In conclusion, the symbiotic relationship between SEITs, solar energy, and commercial enterprises is not just beneficial but essential for fostering a thriving, sustainable future. It's a tripartite win: investors see substantial returns, the environment benefits from cleaner, more sustainable energy solutions, and society at large enjoys the creation of new jobs and a move toward a more responsible and sustainable future. As we look ahead, remember that the future isn't just brighter with solar energy; it's smarter, more sustainable, and within reach with the right guidance and expertise.

The future is not only brighter with solar power but also promises greater financial luminosity!

CHAPTER 5

FEDERAL GRANTS AND FORGIVABLE LOANS

The cost of photovoltaic (PV) solar power has drastically declined over the past decade, making solar the cheapest form of electricity in the United States of America.

This cost competitiveness, combined with a growing awareness of environmental issues, has led to a surge in demand for solar energy worldwide. The global push towards decarbonization and renewable energy targets set by governments further bolsters the solar market. Countries around the world are incentivizing solar energy through tax credits, subsidies, and feed-in tariffs, making investments in solar projects more attractive.

Investing in solar energy presents a unique opportunity to participate in a market that is not only financially rewarding but also contributes to a sustainable future. As the world increasingly turns to renewable energy, solar investments stand out for their growth potential, environmental benefits, and alignment with global energy trends. While challenges exist, the overall outlook for the solar investment landscape is positive, promising a bright future for those willing to tap into this sun-powered opportunity.

Navigating government incentives and grants for solar energy involves understanding various funding opportunities, eligibility criteria, and application processes. These incentives and grants are crucial in making solar energy more accessible and financially viable for a wide range of users, including homeowners, businesses, and non-profit organizations.

Pioneering Sustainable Futures: Harnessing the Power of 2,465 Federal Grants

In the dynamic world of green energy, an extraordinary opportunity awaits businesses, non-profits, educational institutions, and rural governments. This opportunity comes in the form of an impressive array of federal grants. With a staggering total of 2,465 grants available, the federal government is ready to substantially fund initiatives that pivot towards sustainability and green energy.

Navigating this vast sea of grants might seem daunting, but this is where specialized expertise comes into play. Diving deep into the complexities and specificities of these grants, one finds a plethora of options tailored to diverse green energy projects. While exploring each of these 2,465 grants is a formidable challenge, it's a journey worth embarking on for the potential rewards it offers.

The secret to successfully unlocking these opportunities lies in the art of reverse engineering the grant application process. Whether you are the CEO or founder of a business aiming to go green, a local government planning sustainable solutions, or an educational leader aspiring to create eco-friendly campuses at her school, there's a grant specifically suited for your needs.

The Timing is Now

The time is now to secure your solar future!

Given the current political and economic landscape, the need to apply for solar energy grants and forgivable loans is urgent. With the approach of 2025, there's a growing threat of a conservative GOP Congress eliminating green energy grants. The recent budget extension offers a two-year golden window, but this may close with a shift in political power. Currently, we are in an optimal period for businesses, especially smaller and rural ones, to secure over 100% funding for solar energy systems. Larger businesses have access to grants covering up to $500 million in costs to go green. Now is the time to act and capitalize on these opportunities, before the political tide turns.

The second compelling reason to invest in solar right now is the moral responsibility we bear towards our planet.

Solar power is clean, and renewable, and cuts carbon footprints. As businesses, we not only contribute to economies but also shape societal norms. A switch to solar energy is a statement that we care about our environment and are willing to invest in its future. By embracing solar power, we lead by example, encouraging our employees, customers, and other businesses to follow suit.

Finally, electricity rates have skyrocketed nationwide and show no signs of slowing down. Solar power provides energy independence and shields businesses from the volatility of traditional energy prices. Consequently, by switching to solar, consumers and businessmen are not only making an environmentally sound decision but also a financially savvy one.

As we delve deeper into the third point, it's critical to understand the upward trend of electricity rates nationwide. Over the past few years, we've witnessed an alarming escalation in electricity prices, a trend set to continue if the status quo remains. It's not just households feeling the pinch; businesses, too, are bearing the brunt of these skyrocketing costs. These ever-increasing utility bills can erode your bottom line, acting as a constant drain on resources. However, solar energy presents a tangible solution to this growing concern. Once the solar power system is installed, your exposure to fluctuating electricity prices evaporates completely. The sun's energy, in contrast to fossil fuels, is free and inexhaustible. By harnessing solar power, you insulate your business from future price hikes, thus ensuring stability and predictability in your energy costs. This move will prove to be financially prudent, especially if you take advantage of the Inflation Reduction Act and let the government pay for your system.

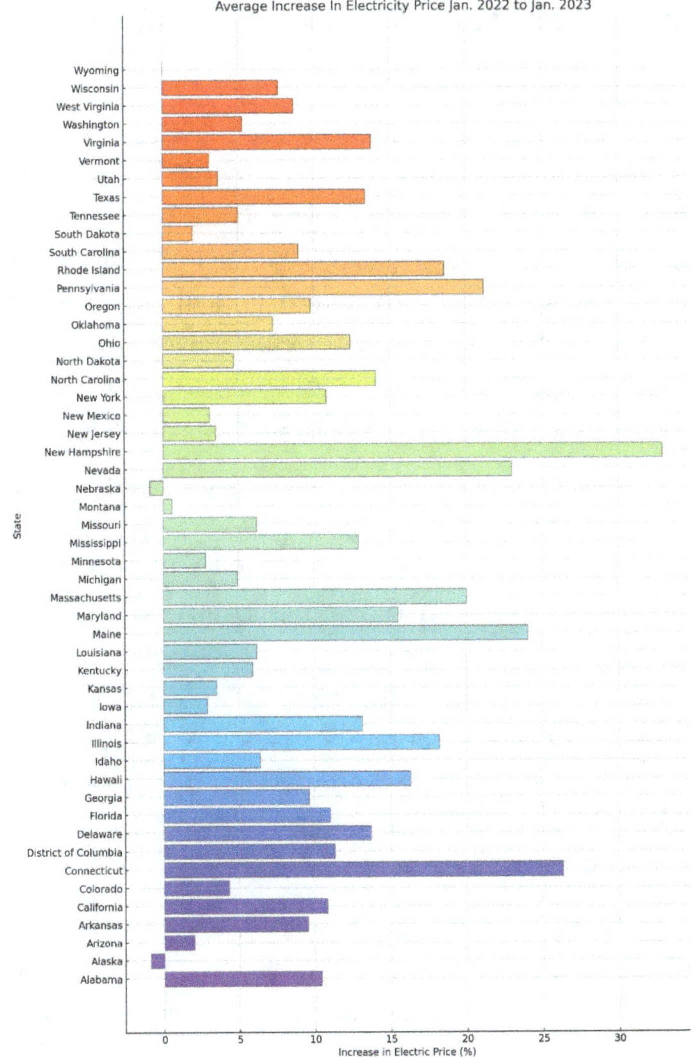

CHAPTER 6

REAP GRANT: SMALL INVESTOR'S GATEWAY TO GOVERNMENT GENEROSITY

In the burgeoning world of green investments and sustainable business practices, the Rural Energy for America Program (REAP) stands as a beacon of opportunity for both small businesses and investors. Designed specifically for those looking to invest a modest seven figures into a Petite solar farm, or for small rural businesses aiming to eradicate their electric bills by going green, REAP offers a powerful incentive.

This unparalleled program, central to this book, is arguably the most significant and advantageous government program for small investors and businessmen seeking to capitalize on green energy incentives. Unlike the vast financial opportunities available to centi-millionaires and billionaires—allowing them to generate hundreds of millions to a billion courtesy of government programs—REAP uniquely caters to the small investor—what I call the *middle-class millionaire businessperson*.

A "*small businessperson*" in this context is defined as someone with a net worth of between $1 million and $25 million. These individuals stand to gain immensely from REAP, potentially securing millions of dollars in free government money.

Let's now dedicate a substantial focus to dissecting and explaining the REAP program, offering a detailed guide on how it can serve as a pivotal tool for your substantial economic gain.

While subsequent chapters will delve into the plethora of excellent government programs available to the ultra-wealthy centi-millionaires and billionaires, it's clear that these opportunities are often beyond the reach of smaller investors with perhaps only a modest seven-figure portfolio to manage and grow.

Therefore, REAP's tailored approach provides a much-needed platform for the aspiring green investor, making it an essential subject for those looking to make a meaningful and profitable venture into sustainable business practices.

What Exactly is the REAP Program?

In this dynamic landscape, REAP serves not just as an incentive, but as a gateway to acquiring up to $1 million in grants. This substantial financial support can cover up to 50% of the costs for a $2 million solar energy system, making it an extraordinarily accessible opportunity for those who qualify. A $2 million Petite Solar Farm could completely revolutionize the way small businesses or investors approach energy consumption and production.

For the small business owner, investing in a $2 million solar farm isn't just an investment in green energy; it's a strategic move to eliminate costly electric bills, leading to significant long-term savings and sustainability. Imagine your business not only contributing to the fight against climate change but also becoming self-sufficient in energy needs.

On the other hand, for the investor, the same $2 million solar farm represents a lucrative opportunity to generate and sell electricity. This isn't just about getting a return on investment through energy sales; it's about contributing to a more sustainable future while also capitalizing on the growing demand for renewable energy.

The REAP grant thus serves as a critical stepping stone for both small business owners and investors to make a substantial impact in the renewable energy sector.

But wait, there's more!

When it comes to financial benefits, the REAP Grant is a force to be reckoned with. The solar energy system not only enjoys a 21% benefit in accelerated depreciation but also qualifies for an investment tax credit (ITC) of 30% to 50%.

The best part?

All these benefits can be stacked, potentially reaching a whopping 121%, effectively making the system a no-brainer investment for REAP businesses.

To make the most of this incredible opportunity, it's important to understand the qualifications.

First and foremost, the solar project must be located in a rural area with a population under 50,000. This covers almost all of the topographical USA, making it accessible to just about everywhere. Even if you live in a big city, chances are there is a rural area not too far away.

Second, The government's approach to green energy incentives is notably directed towards entities and investors with robust financial standing. In essence, these programs are structured to amplify the wealth of those already financially well-established; a millionaire with a net worth of two million might find themselves doubling their worth, just as a woman with $100 million could escalate to $200 million. This trend underscores a fundamental prerequisite for those aspiring to capitalize on such opportunities: a substantial net worth and a solid credit history are critical.

Beyond just having the financial resources, another key qualifier is profitability. To fully leverage these incentives, you must show the financial viability of the project. This creates a synergistic environment where the pursuit of green energy solutions and financial prosperity are not just parallel goals but are deeply interwoven, each propelling the other forward in a mutually beneficial ascent.

Investor Application of REAP: The Investor builds a Petite Solar Farm project for $2 million solar in a rural community and sells the electricity to businesses using a power purchase agreement. The investor offers competitive rates, provides a stable long-term cost, and as investors, apply for a REAP grant which is 50% or $1 million on a $2 million project. When you stack tax credits and other benefits explained herein in this book the investor essentially acquires a $2 million asset for free. This asset becomes a 'cash register' that will generate electricity — essentially cash — for 25 years, underlining the financial viability and sustainability of the investment.

This is the power of leveraging REAP grants as an investor: transforming sunlight into a steady, profitable stream of income while contributing to the community's energy independence.

The beauty of investing in a Petite solar farm through REAP is twofold. Firstly, it allows investors to contribute positively to the environment by providing green energy alternatives to rural businesses and communities. This move not only helps reduce the carbon footprint but also bolsters the local economy by offering cheaper, more stable electricity prices. Secondly, the financial benefits are clear and compelling. The $2 million solar farm stands as a testament to a savvy investment strategy, offering a substantial asset to the investor's portfolio and a reliable income for decades. This approach aligns perfectly with the goals of both the environmentally conscious investor and the profit-driven entrepreneur, making REAP an invaluable tool in the arsenal of anyone looking to make a significant impact in the world of green investments.

CHAPTER 7

STACKING BIDEN'S SUBSTANTIAL TAX CREDITS WITH REAP BENEFITS

Under the Inflation Reduction Act, solar projects, both consumer and commercial, are eligible for significant tax credits. These credits are a form of government incentive that reduces the tax bill of individuals or businesses on a dollar-for-dollar basis. Essentially, if you owe taxes at the end of the year, a tax credit can directly reduce the amount you owe. For consumers and businesses alike, the base tax credit for solar energy projects is 30%, providing a substantial reduction in the overall cost of such initiatives.

However, the tax credits for businesses are notably more generous. Beyond the initial 30%, businesses can qualify for two additional 10% tax credits under certain conditions, such as meeting specific domestic production criteria or installing the solar system in a designated energy community. This means that, potentially, a business could receive up to a 50% tax credit for their solar energy projects, effectively halving the cost of their investment.

What makes these tax credits especially valuable for businesses is their fungibility. There exists a robust market for the buying and selling of tax credits, allowing companies that might not have enough tax liability to fully utilize their credits, or those seeking immediate liquidity, to sell their credits. For instance, if a business qualifies for a $1 million tax credit on a $2 million system, it will be able to convert that credit into cash almost immediately through this market. This aspect of tax credits is particularly beneficial for startups or other companies that are in their early stages and may not yet be profitable or for any business that prefers instant cash flow to a delayed tax benefit. The ability to monetize tax credits provides a level of flexibility and immediate financial benefit that makes investing in solar energy even more attractive and accessible for businesses of all sizes.

Understanding All The Wonderful Tax Credits Available

The basic tax credit under current legislation allows for a substantial 30% reduction in the cost of solar projects for businesses. However, I'm here to guide you on how a business can elevate that benefit from 30% to an impressive 40% or even 50%.

Firstly, it's essential to determine if your business is located in an *"Energy Community."* These are areas designated by the government, often places that have historically been involved in coal, oil, gas, or other non-renewable energy production and are now transitioning to renewable energy sources. If your business operates within one of these Energy Communities, you are eligible for an additional 10%

tax credit. This increase means your business could benefit from a total of 40% in tax credits, significantly reducing the initial cost of your solar energy investment.

This additional incentive is designed to boost economic growth and support the transition to clean energy in areas most affected by the shift away from fossil fuels. It's part of a broader initiative to ensure that the benefits of renewable energy and the move towards a more sustainable future are shared widely and support communities in need of revitalization and new opportunities. So, if your business is in an Energy Community, you're not just investing in the future of your company but also contributing to the larger goal of economic and environmental recovery and sustainability.

What is an energy community?

The government defines these as

1. Brownfield sites,

2. Certain metropolitan and non-metropolitan statistical areas with unemployment rates at or above the national average, and

3. Census tracts where a coal mine closed after 1999. or;

4. A coal-fired electric generating unit retired after 2009.

The concept of "Energy Communities" is a game-changer in the renewable energy sector. These communities encompass a wide range of areas, including states like Kentucky, Arizona, and large parts of Nevada. Even most of Alaska, Southern California, and parts of Michigan and Pennsylvania fall under this category. The list is extensive, covering about one-third of the USA. I encourage you to take a look at the government map online and see for yourself. The selection is vast and the opportunities are abundant.

Having attended numerous government webinars and actively engaging with the C-Suite government executives spearheading these renewable energy programs, the message from the top is unequivocal: Uncle Sam is deeply committed to allocating substantial funding to advance the green energy agenda, especially in rural areas and designated energy communities. This commitment is reflected in the escalating incentives and financial support available to businesses and investors willing to partake in this sustainable shift. For investors, particularly, the benefits stemming from these additional government incentives are substantial and not to be underestimated.

Indeed, for investors, the additional 10% tax credit available in Energy Communities significantly boosts the initial return on investment (ROI), making it an exceptionally attractive proposition. This enhanced incentive effectively decreases the upfront cost of solar projects, directly improving the profitability and appeal of these investments. It's a substantial benefit that not only accelerates the payback period but also increases the overall financial returns of green energy projects. Such a boost in initial ROI is a compelling reason for investors to focus on these designated areas, aligning financial goals with the broader mission of promoting sustainable energy solutions in communities that are transitioning towards a greener future. The opportunity to gain an extra 10% in initial ROI is indeed a wonderful incentive, underlining the government's commitment to making renewable energy investments more accessible and rewarding.

The message is clear: there are significant gains to be made for those who align with the government's green energy initiatives, with substantial support and incentives on offer to make these investments more lucrative and impactful.

Go USA And Investors Get An Additional 10%

Introducing the Domestic Content Adder – a thrilling new incentive that grants an additional 10% Investment Tax Credit (ITC) if you use (at least some) domestic products in your solar project. You read that right – a whopping 10% extra just for going local. This incredible incentive takes solar project benefits to an entirely new level.

With the new Domestic Content Adder, you could be looking at an astronomical 121% return on investment! That is what makes this Domestic Content added even more attractive - - that is the ability to stack this new 10% adder with other grants or forgivable loans.

However, like any new policy, this recent addition comes with a fair share of questions and uncertainties. While mom-and-pop solar companies are excitedly touting the benefits, there's a need for clarity in interpreting the law's wording. The law states that if you use American steel and at least 40% American-made products, you qualify for the additional 10% ITC. But what happens if a U.S.-made solar panel contains a small component, like a wire, manufactured in China? This is where things become less clear, and the IRS is expected to issue detailed guidance shortly.

Adding to the intrigue, the law also stipulates that if using foreign products would increase costs by 25% or more compared to U.S. products, you can still qualify for the extra 10%.

But how do you prove that, and what does it mean?

These are questions that the government is working on answering, but the bottom line is that this new credit has incredible potential.

It is particularly exciting that the Domestic Product Tax Credit offers an additional financial boost to those who invest in American-made materials. By utilizing USA-made solar panels and iron in their solar projects, businesses availing themselves of another 10% tax credit, elevate the total potential credit to an impressive 40% (non-energy community) and even

50% in energy communities like Sun Rich Texas that offers the best of all worlds (sun and the best ROI).

This tax credit is substantial, encouraging businesses to support local manufacturing while benefiting financially. However, it's crucial to understand the intricacies and current interpretations of this incentive. As of this writing, the criteria set by the IRS are stringent, with the potential to disqualify a project over minute details, such as a small component of a solar panel not being made in the USA. Some companies are navigating these regulations successfully, but there's a general sense that the current stipulations are overly restrictive, potentially undermining the incentive's intent.

Given the government's overall generous stance towards solar energy and the current administration's commitment to renewable initiatives, there's optimism that the IRS will address these practical issues. It's reasonable to anticipate that the guidelines will evolve to make credit more accessible while still supporting domestic production.

I encourage you to follow me on LinkedIn for the latest updates and insights. I am committed to navigating these complexities on behalf of my clients, aiming to secure the full range of credits available. While there are no guarantees until the IRS provides more definitive guidance, the trajectory suggests a favorable resolution. Keep informed and be prepared to capitalize on these incentives as they become more attainable.

CHAPTER 8

Maximizing Solar Investments with Accelerated Depreciation

Under the Inflation Reduction Act, one of the significant benefits offered to businesses investing in renewable energy projects, like solar energy, is accelerated depreciation. Accelerated depreciation is a tax incentive that allows businesses to write off the cost of an asset more quickly than the asset's actual life expectancy. Instead of spreading the cost of the asset over its entire useful life, accelerated depreciation lets businesses deduct a larger portion of the asset's cost in the early years following the investment. This method of depreciation is particularly beneficial for assets that might become outdated quickly or lose value faster than standard wear and tear.

For a solar energy project, accelerated depreciation means that a company can deduct the majority, if not all, of the cost of the solar system from their taxable income much sooner than they normally would.

Here's how the math works: suppose your business invests in a $1 million solar energy project. With depreciation, you can deduct the entire $1 million, generally over a five-year period (albeit your CPA may be able to accelerate this!)!

If your corporate tax rate is 21%, this deduction can lead to $210,000 in tax savings. Essentially, accelerated depreciation provides a substantial tax shield and improves cash flow in the early years following the investment.

It's important to note that while accelerated depreciation significantly reduces taxable income, it does not generate a tax credit. Unlike tax credits that directly reduce the amount of tax you owe dollar for dollar, depreciation only reduces the amount of income subject to tax. However, the immediate and substantial reduction in taxable income can significantly improve a business's financial position and return on investment, especially in the initial years following the investment.

One key aspect to remember is that accelerated depreciation cannot be sold like tax credits. It's a deduction that applies directly to the business that invested and is utilizing the asset. If the deduction creates a net operating loss, some businesses may have the option to carry forward these losses to offset taxable income in future years, further reducing tax liabilities down the line. However, the specific rules and opportunities around carrying forward depreciation deductions can be complex and vary depending on the business's financial situation and tax profile. Therefore, it's crucial to consult with a certified public accountant (CPA) or a tax professional who can provide guidance tailored to your business's unique circumstances and help you maximize the benefits of accelerated depreciation for your solar energy project. They can help navigate the intricate tax implications and ensure compliance with all relevant tax laws, making the most of this valuable incentive.

CHAPTER 9

CASE STUDY: *PETITE SOLAR FARM,* $1M MINIMUM INVESTMENT, EXCEPTIONAL EBITDA

Welcome to a groundbreaking investment opportunity, tailored specifically for small investors who only can invest a modest seven figures. This chapter is designed to navigate you through the intricacies and review the benefits, and substantial potential returns of such an investment, ensuring you have all the information needed to make an informed and lucrative decision.

Imagine building your own *Petite Solar Farm*, where the bulk of your investment is rebated through government grants and incentives, transforming your expenditure into a sun-powered cash register. As the owner of this eco-friendly enterprise, you'll sell the generated electricity directly to retail clients via Power Purchase Agreements (PPAs).

This direct-to-consumer approach is not just profitable, but astoundingly so, offering returns potentially 500% to 600% higher than selling to the grid. In essence, while selling to the grid is profitable, selling directly to consumers is an opportunity of wonderfully delicious proportions, making this venture not just a smart environmental choice, but also an exceptionally rewarding financial investment.

Reviewing the Investment Potential in REAP and Energy Communities

The Rural Energy for America Program (REAP) is a cornerstone for investors looking to dive into the solar energy market, offering a substantial return of 50% of project costs in grant form. Targeting REAP communities, which are predominantly areas with populations under 50,000, aligns with an investor's best interest due to the widespread geographical availability across the United States.

In addition to the lucrative 50% grant, investors can expect a standard 30% Investment Tax Credit (ITC) on their solar projects. By choosing U.S.-made products, there's a potential to add another 10% ITC, further enhancing the investment's attractiveness. If the project is located within an Energy Community, a designation covering roughly 30% of U.S. geography, investors unlock an additional 10% ITC. This cumulative financial incentive makes solar investment increasingly viable and profitable.

Furthermore, the Inflation Reduction Act allows for the entire cost of the solar project to be depreciated over just five years. This accelerated depreciation translates into another 21% of government-backed financial benefits for profitable corporate entities.

Here's a shark simple formula: "Location, Location, Incentivation!" The savvy investor zeroes in on project locations that double-dip in financial incentives by qualifying as both a REAP and an Energy Community. This strategy isn't just smart; it's a direct line to maximizing returns in the solar energy market.

Locations like Texas and Arizona are not only REAP and Energy Community eligible but also offer the added advantage of high solar irradiance. This means more sunlight and, consequently, more energy production from your solar farm, leading to more bang for your buck. By strategically placing solar investments in these areas, investors can maximize the production capability of their solar farms, ensuring a higher yield and a quicker return on investment. This smart geographical selection, combined with the substantial financial incentives available, makes investing in solar energy a highly attractive and profitable venture. The bottom line is clear: for those looking to invest in solar energy, leveraging the combination of REAP and Energy Community benefits in high-sunlight areas is a strategy that promises enhanced returns and accelerated profitability.

Let's clarify and underscore the potential returns: In an Energy Community that also qualifies for REAP, the incentives combined offer an astounding 121% return based on the cost of the project. Outside of these Energy Communities but still within REAP-eligible areas, the return remains impressive at 111%. These figures aren't just abstract percentages; they represent a full recoupment of your initial $2 million investment and even more, thanks to the government's incentives.

Here's how it breaks down: you invest $1 million to build a Petite Solar Farm. Through a combination of grants and tax incentives - including the 50% REAP grant, 30% standard Investment Tax Credit (ITC), possible additional 10% for using U.S.-made products, another 10% for being in an Energy Community, and the benefits from accelerated depreciation - you're not just getting your initial investment back. You're essentially being paid to make this investment, ending up with more than what you put in (albeit your grant benefit is considered taxable income).

But the return doesn't stop at just getting your money back. Once the project is complete, you own a $1 million asset - a productive, income-generating Petite Solar Farm. This asset not only continues to produce electricity (which you can sell, turning sunlight into revenue) but also stands as a valuable piece of capital. Should you choose, you could leverage this asset further by selling it, passing on the benefits of the solar farm's cash-generating capabilities to another buyer while enjoying the lucrative return on your initial investment. Thus, the investment in a REAP and Energy Community qualifying solar project isn't just about the considerable immediate return; it's about creating and owning an asset that keeps on giving.

Sustainable Investment in Action

Let's delve into a real-life scenario to understand the investor benefits. Imagine Bill, who owns a hotel in a REAP-designated area (non-Energy Community) in Connecticut. His hotel incurs an annual electric bill of $60,000, translating to $5,000 monthly.

Under our model, we would lock in a fixed monthly rate of $5,000 for 25 years for Bill. This approach not only offers Bill a consistent rate, safeguarding against fluctuating energy costs but also aligns with environmentally conscious practices. For the investor, this translates to securing a Power Purchase Agreement (PPA) worth $60,000 gross annually over 25 years.

In this example, before commencing any construction you first secure your grant approval limiting potential exposure to you as an investor. After the grant is approved you start product procurement and construction installation. You either need to finance or pay the $1 million cost upfront. This is because the construction must be finalized before the government will pay out the funds for your pre-approved grant. Typically, grant funds are disbursed around 30 days after the project is operational and has passed a government inspection confirming it meets specified standards outlined in the grant application.

The timeline from breaking ground to completion can vary; however, for planning purposes, let's consider six months as a worst-case scenario for a small Petite

Solar Farm. The financial cost of financing the $1 million over these six months is estimated to be 3.5%, which adds $35,000 to the overall project costs.

In this non-energy community scenario, the tax credit amounts to $400,000 (40%). If your corporate entity is unable to utilize the tax credit, or if you prefer immediate liquidity, this credit is transferable and can typically be sold for about $360,000.

Thus, you initially invest $1 million and, within six months, effectively receive $860,000 back for the system. After accounting for the cost of financing, this amount reduces to $825,000, leaving your net outlay at $175,000.

The grant amount you receive for the project is taxable income. If your business is a corporation, this means you could be taxed at up to 21% on the grant amount. However, there's a beneficial aspect to consider: accelerated depreciation. Under the Inflation Reduction Act, you depreciate 20% of the project's cost each year for five years.

In practical terms, let's say you receive a $500,000 grant. Based on the maximum corporate tax rate of 21%, you would owe $105,000 in taxes. However, with accelerated depreciation, you can deduct $200,000 each year for five years from your taxable income, which is 20% of the $1 million project cost. This deduction in the first year significantly reduces the tax burden from the grant. Over five years, the total accelerated depreciation amounts to $1 million, equating to $200,000 per year, effectively giving you a net gain of $105,000 in tax savings over the life of the project.

However, there's a catch with the recovery period of the accelerated depreciation, as it doesn't immediately offset the entire tax on the grant. In the first year, you still owe $105,000, but you'll only receive a tax saving of $42,000, leaving a net amount of $63,000 due in taxes. If you carry this balance for one year, the cost, considering an average interest rate, would be about $4,400. Adding a modest interest charge for the period before your accelerated depreciation benefits fully offset the tax on the grant, the total cost of carrying this negative balance can be roughly estimated at around $5,500.

Remember, initially, your out-of-pocket expense was $175,000 after accounting for grants and selling your tax credits. If you had utilized your tax credit directly instead of selling it, your outlay would have been reduced to $135,000. However, for this example, let's proceed with the $175,000 figure.

Now, taking into account the benefits from accelerated depreciation and factoring in the tax on the grant, you effectively recover $105,000. This means that your net cost for purchasing the $1 million solar energy system is now down to $70,000. And if you had used the tax credits yourself, the cost would further decrease to $30,000.

After considering the tax implications of these "free" incentives, the real cost translates to a nominal three to seven cents on the dollar for your seven-figure investment in a solar energy system. This means that for every dollar spent, only a small fraction is the actual cost to you, turning a substantial investment into an economically viable and nearly free source of renewable energy.

EBITDA

The economic feasibility of this solar project is largely dependent on establishing a Power Purchase Agreement (PPA) with retail buyers. To put this into perspective, let's consider the example of a hotel project above. Here, it's projected that the hotel would contribute $60,000 annually for the solar energy supplied. Out of this, I or any legitimate promoter would charge a Royalty for securing the PPA of 25% of gross or $15,000 per annum. Additionally, the project will incur $5,000 annually for maintenance. This arrangement leads to an annual annuity, of $40,000 for the investor When you juxtapose this against the post-incentive project costs, which lie between $30,000 and $70,000, the return on investment appears quite remarkable.

This Gets Even Juicer

The REAP Grant offers additional intriguing aspects that are worth considering, especially the government's 1.4 rule and the method of calculating solar output.

Under the rules of the REAP Grant, the grant and its associated benefits cover systems that produce up to 1.4 times the electric usage of a company subject to the PPA. This rule opens up a range of strategic possibilities. For instance, an investment company can opt to 'overbuild' its solar energy system relative to its immediate energy needs. This overbuilding allows the company not only to meet its energy requirements but also to generate excess electricity.

The potential to sell this excess electricity creates another attractive opportunity. For businesses with suitable premises, setting up electric vehicle (EV) charging stations could be a viable option. By doing so, a company can use its overbuilt capacity to power these charging stations, creating a new revenue stream. This approach aligns well with the increasing adoption of EVs and the growing need for accessible charging solutions.

Another Benefit: The Government Uses Conservative Numbers

Another crucial facet of the REAP program concerns the calculation of solar output for Petite Solar Farms. Under REAP guidelines, when you apply for a grant the estimation of solar energy production for your project, relies on government-provided data. This data reflects the average sunlight exposure for solar panels in specific locations. These government figures used to calculate the solar output are typically very conservative.

In practice, your is likely to produce more energy than these estimates suggest, offering a potentially higher yield than initially projected.

Note

Although the figures provided here are accurate and represent a realistic example of a successful investment in a Petite Solar Farm, it's important to recognize that these numbers are primarily illustrative. They are intended to highlight the potential opportunities and outcomes in such investments, rather than guarantee specific results.

CHAPTER 10

43 REAP Q&As: Essential Insights for Solar Investment Success

In this chapter, we supercharge your knowledge with the top 43 frequently asked questions about the REAP Program! In previous chapters, we've illuminated how small businesses and investors in rural areas can harness a staggering ROI of up to 121% in government benefits for solar energy systems priced up to $2 million.

REAP is the pinnacle of the Joe Biden giveaway under the Inflation Reduction Act. Despite enlightening the public with newsletters and a plethora of educational material, the questions kept coming into my inbox.

So here I am, ready to dive into this 43-question treasure trove, ensuring your journey to a sun-powered future, generously sponsored by Uncle Sam, is crystal clear!

1. Q: What are the Criteria for Determining Maximum Grant Funding?

    A: Applications post-April 1, 2023, are eligible for up to 50% federal grants if they involve zero-emission renewable systems, are in Energy Communities, focus on energy efficiency, or are proposed by Tribal entities. All other projects have a limit of 25%. This differentiation ensures a balanced approach to various types of projects while prioritizing environmentally impactful initiatives.

2. Q: Are Anaerobic Digesters and Biogas Projects Eligible for the 50% Federal Grant Share?

A: Yes, these projects qualify for a 50% grant if they're within an Energy Community or proposed by a Tribal entity. This inclusion underlines the program's commitment to innovative, sustainable energy solutions, especially in communities and groups focused on environmental stewardship.

3. Q: Do Net Zero or Negative GHGS Projects Qualify for the 50% Federal Grant Share?

A: Projects with net zero or negative GHGS are eligible for the 50% grant only if located in an Energy Community or proposed by Tribal entities. This emphasizes the importance of location and the nature of the proposing entity in determining grant eligibility, with a clear preference for projects that have a substantial environmental impact.

4. Q: What is the Meaning of 'At the Project Level' in Terms of Emissions?

   A: 'At the project level' refers to considering only the direct emissions from the project site, excluding external or indirect emissions. This approach allows for a more focused assessment of a project's environmental impact.

5. Q: What is the Maximum Amount for Grant Requests?

   A: Applicants can request up to $500,000 for energy efficiency improvements and $1 million for renewable energy systems, with no cap on the total project size. This provides significant financial support for substantial projects, enabling more comprehensive and impactful energy solutions.

6. Q: Is There a Limit on the Number of REAP Applications Per Fiscal Year?

   A: Yes, an applicant is limited to one renewable energy system (RES) and one energy efficiency improvement (EEI) application per fiscal year, with a cap of $1.5 million in total grant assistance. This ensures a fair distribution of funds among applicants.

7. Q: How is an 'Energy Community' Defined?

   A: Defined in 26 U.S.C. 45 (b)(11)(B), an Energy Community is determined by the Department of Energy, focusing on areas impacted by changes in the energy sector. This definition plays a crucial role in prioritizing funding for communities transitioning towards renewable energy.

8. Q: What are the Deadlines for REAP Grant Applications and the ComPetition Process?

A: REAP features six quarterly application windows, with applications competing by score in the subsequent quarter. Grant requests of $20,000 or less have a dedicated set-aside, and applications first compete for state allocation, followed by national pooling. Unfunded applications automatically enter the next competition but must be withdrawn if not funded by the fiscal year-end.

9. Q: How does the combined grant and guaranteed loan application process work in REAP?

A: It's seamless! Apply for both grants and loans simultaneously, anytime during the year. If your grant shines through, the loan funds are reserved, making it a win-win!

10. Q: Can a project be funded by both REAP and NRCS EQIP?

A: Yes, but remember, the total federal grant share, combining REAP and EQIP, can't exceed 50%. This keeps the funding fair and balanced.

11. Q: Is it possible to combine a REAP grant with the Federal 30% Investment Tax Credit?

> A: Absolutely! Dive into both incentives without worry. The tax credit, different from a grant, reduces taxable income post-installation.

12. Q: Is the REAP grant considered taxable income?

> A: Yes, it's taxable. Successful applicants will receive a Form 1099-G for tax purposes.

13. Q: Can new businesses without historical energy consumption apply for REAP?

> A: New ventures can apply for renewable energy projects, scored as energy generation.

14. Q: Are rural electric and housing cooperatives eligible for REAP?

> A: If they meet the SBA size standards, they're in! Just ensure the improvements don't benefit residential quarters.

15. Q: What about munis and small business eligibility for REAP?

> A: Munis are eligible if they serve rural areas and operate independently. For small businesses, it's about meeting the SBA's size standards.

16. Q: Are 501C3 Non-Profits Eligible for REAP?

> A: Generally, no. But there are exceptions! Think cooperatives, electric utilities, tribal

business entities, and agricultural producers. They just need to fit into the small business category as defined in the regulations.

17. Q: Can Hemp Farms Apply for REAP?

A: Yes, but with conditions. Hemp projects need state licenses and USDA-approved plans. Remember, REAP steers clear of hemp used for nutritional or medicinal purposes, including CBD.

18. Q: Are Marijuana Grow Operations Eligible for REAP?

A: No, they're off the table. Despite state legality, federal law keeps them ineligible for REAP.

19. Q: What about Multiple Renewable Energy Systems Across States?

A: One entity, multiple locations? File one application if the technology (like solar PV) is consistent across sites. Mixing tech? Pick one for the application. Remember, each site needs its environmental review.

20. Q: Eligibility of Standalone Battery Storage and EV Charging Stations?

A: Standalone batteries are a no-go. But retrofitting an existing renewable system with a battery? That's a yes! EV charging stations?

Only if they're part of a renewable system and not for retail use.

21. Q: What about Wind Turbines and Solar Tractors?

A: REAP supports commercially available wind turbines but says no to solar tractors and other electrified vehicles.

22. Q: Definition of an 'Eligible Rural Area' for REAP?

A: A rural area as defined in the regulations. Projects in non-rural corporate headquarters are eligible if the project site is rural. Agricultural producers get more leeway – their projects can be in non-rural areas if they're tied to onsite agricultural production.

23. Q: What Defines an Energy Efficiency Improvement in REAP?

A: Think green upgrades! Energy efficiency in REAP means revamping or replacing your building, systems, or equipment to cut down annual energy use. It's all about proving the savings through an energy audit. From lighting to HVAC, if it's more efficient, it's in.

24. Q: Can New Buildings Fit into REAP's Energy Efficiency Category?

A. For new constructions, it's a no. REAP focuses on upgrading existing structures for energy efficiency. However, agricultural producers have a unique path with guaranteed loans for new energy-efficient systems.

25. Q: What's REAP's Stance on Renewable Energy and Green Hydrogen Systems?

A: Renewable energy in REAP is all about natural forces like wind, sun, and water. Green hydrogen systems using water and solar? They're in!

26. Q: Are Air Source Heat Pumps REAP-Friendly?

A: Yes, as long as they show real energy savings. They're part of the energy efficiency family but not the renewable category.

27. Q: Do You Need Past Energy Data for Renewable Projects?

A: Not for new installations. REAP supports new renewable energy systems, like a fresh geothermal setup for a new building, scoring it as energy generation.

28. Q: What About Home-Based Businesses and Residential Units for REAP?

A: REAP draws the line at residential use. Home businesses, apartment complexes, and similar setups aren't eligible because measuring their energy contribution gets too tricky.

29. Q: Handling Shared Meters in Renewable Energy Projects?

> A: Got a shared meter at your farmstead? Your project is good to go if at least half of the energy benefits your business. It's about balancing the energy books between home and business use.

30. Q: Are Lease-to-Own or Capitalized Leases Eligible in REAP?

> A: No, full ownership is key. REAP projects need to be wholly owned and operated by the applicant, not just leased.

31. Q: What Does Site Control Mean for REAP Applicants?

> A: Control is crucial. Applicants must have command over the project site for its entire useful life. Don't own it? A long-term lease with the site owner is essential.

32. Q: When Can Costs be Incurred in a REAP Project?

> A: Timing is everything. Costs before the award announcement come with risks. Only expenses post-application are covered. And remember, environmental reviews are a must before starting construction.

33. Q: Is Buying Land Covered Under REAP?

A: Land purchase? Yes, but only with REAP's guaranteed loan program, not with grants.

34. Q: What Costs are Eligible in REAP Projects?

A: Think direct project fees. Interconnection, licensing, and permit fees post-application are eligible, but pre-application fees like energy audits or engineering studies aren't.

35. Q: How are Changes in Project Costs Handled?

A: Keep your budget in check. The grant is based on initial project costs. Increase in costs? No extra funds. Decrease? The grant might shrink too.

36. Q: Can REAP Fund Roof Costs for Solar Installations?

A: Only if the roof is being adapted for the installation. New construction roofs? That's a no. But a carport for a solar charging station? That's a green light.

37. Q: Does BABAA Apply to REAP Grants?

A: Only for specific non-Federal entities, infrastructure projects involving construction.

38. Q: Are Davis Bacon Wage Rates Relevant to REAP?

A: No, they don't apply here.

39. Q: Is a Feasibility Study Mandatory for All Renewable Energy Projects in REAP?

A: No, it's project-specific. Solar PV? Usually, there is no need. But a complex biomass project? A feasibility study might be on the cards. Check with your State Energy Coordinator.

40. Q: Do All REAP Applicants Need SAM Registration?

A: Absolutely! Register in SAM and grab that Unique Entity Identification Number. Struggling with registration? Document your efforts, and you might still be in the game.

41. Q: Are Energy Assessments Required for All Energy Efficiency Projects?

A: Yes, indeed. Show those energy savings based on your history to qualify.

42. Q: What Environmental Review Documents are Needed for REAP Applications?

A: It varies, so connect with your State Coordinator. At a minimum, your application should include comprehensive environmental information.

43. Q: How to Identify if a Project is in a Disadvantaged or Distressed Community for Extra Points?

> A: Check out the USDA's map tool for the scoop. It'll guide you in pinpointing if your project is in one of these communities.

Seize Solar Wealth: REAP's A Million-Dollar Miracle for Your Business or Investment Portfolio!

CHAPTER 11

AMAZEMENT

I've stumbled upon a narrative so baffling it makes refusing free front-row tickets to the greatest concert of the year look downright rational. Here's the kicker: A CEO, ensconced in the plush corner office of a REAP-designated enterprise, dared to contemplate the government's lavish REAP program. And then, brace yourselves – with a level of nonchalance that could make a cat nod in approval, he decided not to do it.

Now, I have to wonder: is his bank account bursting at the seams with all that excess cash?

Think about it. The government is, in no uncertain terms, handing out a golden ticket to curb his hefty electric bills, and this maestro is humming and hawing. A seven-figure system, largely footed by the government, that could slice and dice his monthly energy costs – what's the conundrum here? Is he genuinely contemplating the pros and cons or just indulging in some high-stakes financial Russian roulette?

His mental gymnastics must be something else: "*A government-backed opportunity to drastically cut down on expenses and invest in the future? Eh, maybe it's too mainstream for my avant-garde entrepreneurial spirit.*"

End of the day, if overflowing bank accounts and the thrill of wasting potential savings is the new CEO flex, then more power to this trendsetter. But, between you and me, in a world where a penny saved is a penny earned, such decisions deserve their reality show. It'd be comedy gold!

Here's the scene for those who've been living under a financially savvy rock: If your business resides in a quaint rural area, with population figures that don't breach the 50,000 mark, and you're regularly dishing out anything between $500 and $50,000 monthly on electric bills, Uncle Sam is quite literally extending an olive branch made of dollar bills. We're talking up to $1 million in grants, which translates to the government covering half of a $2 million solar system installation. It's like walking into a luxury car showroom and being told, "Pick any car, you'll only pay for the air freshener."

So, to our esteemed CEO, who flirted with financial brilliance only to swipe left on it, I have to ask: Is your bank account filled with too much excess cash?

Summing up this saga of unfathomable choices: The government is pretty much setting a platter of golden incentives at your feet. But I guess some folks just have a unique appetite. Here's to hoping the next story I tell is of CEOs running, not walking, to these opportunities.

CHAPTER 12

The Centi-Millionaire's Dive: Shark Tank Strategies

Imagine being one of only 28,420 individuals who have a net worth exceeding $100 million. Now picture the U.S. Government presenting you with a magnificent gift: a sprawling *Grande Solar Farm* valued at $100 million. This isn't just a purchase; it's a significant asset granted to you, a testament to your status among the country's elite centi-millionaires.

This isn't just any investment; it's akin to being gifted a wealth-generating machine, a testament to your status and financial acumen. The government extends extraordinary offers like this, recognizing your economic stature, allowing you to substantially increase your net worth and continue reaping benefits for 25 years. *The Grande Solar Farm* isn't merely an asset; it's a powerhouse converting sunlight into a continuous stream of income, all underpinned by the sun's unyielding vigor.

This transcends imagination into a vivid opportunity, framed by significant governmental incentives tailored for an elite few. With grants, forgivable loans, and tax credits, the government essentially finances this venture, turning your solar farm into a fountain of profit. The investment is not just in solar panels but in a future of sustained wealth creation, leveraging renewable energy for lucrative returns. It's a crystal-clear proposition: harness the sun, capitalize on governmental support, and watch as your *Grand Solar Farm* transforms into a perpetual money-minting machine, securing your financial legacy for decades.

An Investment For A Shark's Shark

Imagine an opportunity that, while not fitting the usual profile featured on "Shark Tank," represents the pinnacle of strategic investments for centi-millionaires, billionaires, and the savvy Sharks themselves. Despite straying from the typical entrepreneurial pitches on the show, the construction of a *Grande Solar Farm* is a financial venture that commands attention due to its immense potential.

By investing $100 million into the creation of a *Grande Solar Farm*, these affluent investors wouldn't just be spending their money; they would be positioning themselves to recoup their entire investment—and more—through government incentives. But the true financial powerhouse here isn't just the recovery of the initial outlay. When these investors secure retail power purchase agreements (PPAs), they unlock the capability of their solar farm to generate up to $45 million in annual gross revenue (based on a $100 million farm under prime conditions). This is significantly more lucrative than selling power back to the grid, as utility companies typically pay less—a mere fifth—of the potential earnings from direct retail sales.

The real treasure of this investment lies in forging long-term PPAs with retail clients, effectively sidestepping utility companies. It's about building a renewable energy empire that delivers a high yield, not just in energy but in revenue, making it an investment that could be too grand for the "Shark Tank" stage, yet perfect for a Shark's portfolio.

Deep Dive Admiration: Why I'm Hooked on the Sharks of *Shark Tank*

Each episode of 'Shark Tank' is like a masterclass in entrepreneurship, and I find myself in awe of the Sharks' acumen and expertise. Their sharp instincts for innovation and their strategic business maneuvers are not just entertaining but incredibly educational. I admire their boldness in investment decisions, their ability to see potential in budding entrepreneurs, and their commitment to mentorship. These titans of industry have a knack for cutting through the noise to find the real value in a business proposition. Their diverse backgrounds contribute to a rich tapestry of business wisdom that I, along with countless others, love to watch unfold. It's the combination of their shrewd deal-making skills and their passion for fostering growth that cements my respect and admiration for all the Sharks.

Beyond the Ring: No 'Shark Tank' Product Has Made the Sharks Billions—Yet

While Shark Tank's glitz and glamor have showcased countless innovations, it often favors the unconventional and the one-of-a-kind. Pitching something as everyday as water? The Sharks might dismissively swim away within seconds. However, Zhong Shanshan defied expectations. Rather than leveraging the latest technological innovation, he tapped into the universal necessity of water and developed a $62 billion net worth simply by bottling and selling it - - water that is!

Now, imagine harnessing something even more prevalent than water, teeming with boundless potential. Yes, I'm talking about electricity. As common as it is, every home, every device, every industry depends on it. Much like Zhong's success with water, the real billion-dollar opportunities often lie in these common commodities.

Yet, there's a nuance to consider: Diving deep into these governmental incentives in renewable energy requires more than a mere vision of solar farms and green ventures. It demands formidable financial strength and a pristine reputation, the hallmarks of a true Shark. In essence, it's akin to corporate welfare where the government aims to elevate those already soaring high. If you can't stand tall among industry giants, the doors of vetting remain closed. Simply put, it's a realm reserved for the elite, and only a select few have the privilege to access its bounty.

An Irresistible Investment For A Shark

Why This Makes Perfect Cents (and Dollars)

- Math & Magic: With the government covering significant portions of the costs, every watt generated becomes a nugget of profit. This isn't just a good ROI; it's astronomical.

- Partially forgivable PACE loans, where up to 40% of your $100 million is magically wiped away, provide centi-millionaires with the ultimate government gift. Imagine crafting a $100 million solar farm and having 40% of that sum simply... evaporate. The result? Premium infrastructure at dime-store costs.

- Stacking Benefits: The grants and forgivable loans offered to construct a *Grande Solar Farm* are stackable with tax credits and sometimes also stackable with forgivable loans. While this intricate dance might be a little tricky for smaller projects, the government benefits are worth it, often surpassing 111% of the cost of the project.

So, to the 35 Sharks of Shark Tank, and the grand army of 28,420 centi-millionaires in the USA (also Sharks, but not celebrity Sharks), this isn't just an invitation; it's a challenge. Only the likes of you, the apex elite, can navigate these waters and access the $100 million (in some cases as much as $500 million) treasure that the government has set aside as a special gift for you. Get a reserved seat at a table where fortunes are made. Not everyone gets a ticket, but then again, not everyone is a Shark or a centi-millionaire.

To sum it up: If this investment were any hotter, we'd need a solar panel just to handle it. Let Zhong Shanshan's success be a beacon, illuminating the limitless potential in tapping into everyday essentials. This is your exclusive invitation to explore the vast and verdant landscape of green energy.

Solar Farms: The Ultimate Shark Investment Explained

Owning any size solar farm is akin to owning a machine that prints money powered by none other than the mighty sun. As tantalizing as this sounds, it's no fantasy.

The allure of this proposal lies in the substantial governmental backing. For any investment, especially in a solar venture, the numbers need to align favorably. Yet, when the government steps in, covering a significant fraction or even the entirety of the costs through grants, forgivable loans, and tax credits, the potential return on investment becomes genuinely staggering.

Just What is a *Grande Solar Farm*?

Grande Solar Farms are large-scale (usually 100 Mega-Watts in size or larger) installations comprising photovoltaic (PV) panels that capture and convert sunlight into clean, renewable electricity. These farms play a quintessential role in reducing fossil fuel reliance, minimizing greenhouse gas emissions, and supporting the grid during peak demand. The electricity generated can either be sold directly to consumers or fed into the local electricity grid (for a reduced amount), ensuring a steady revenue stream for investors.

The Solar Bounty of Texas

Selecting a prime location for a solar farm is a strategic move that requires careful consideration of several factors, including sunlight exposure and local weather patterns. Texas, with its expansive blue skies, has become an increasingly attractive option for such ventures. The state boasts an impressive average of 11 hours of sunlight per day, which means more potential energy capture for solar panels. This abundant sunshine isn't just about quantity; it's also about quality. The sun's intensity in Texas is particularly strong, significantly boosting the efficiency and output of solar farms.

However, potential investors like our Shark Tank aficionados must also weigh the risks. Texas is no stranger to extreme weather events like hail and tornadoes, which can pose threats to the integrity of solar installations. Nevertheless, these risks can be mitigated. The market offers comprehensive insurance policies designed specifically for solar farms, providing robust protection against these natural events. With such insurance solutions, the risks associated with

Texas' weather can be managed, ensuring that the solar farm remains a sound investment.

For a Shark who's accustomed to navigating the rough seas of business, Texas presents a compelling opportunity. Its solar-friendly climate, when paired with the right protective measures, can yield a high return on investment, transforming natural sunlight into a renewable and profitable energy source. This aligns well with the savvy business strategies often seen on Shark Tank, where calculated risks are embraced for greater rewards.

Additionally, Texas operates as a free electric market, offering a unique advantage where one can directly secure a retail client and sell electricity to them, bypassing the traditional grid. This direct-to-consumer model enhances the potential profitability of the solar farm by removing the middleman, allowing for more competitive pricing and better margins. This business model is an attractive proposition for investors looking to maximize their returns in the renewable energy space.

Finally, as I discussed in this book previously as an additional incentive for solar farm investment in Texas, it's important to note that most of the state qualifies as an energy community. This means the government offers an enticing 10% tax credit on such renewable energy projects. For a $100 million solar farm, this isn't just a slight boost but a substantial $10 million contribution, courtesy of government incentives. This significant tax credit further enhances the financial appeal of establishing a solar farm in Texas, making the sunny state an even brighter prospect for savvy investors.

Delving into the Math

In our case study, we explore the construction of a Solar Farm in Texas, strategically located within an energy community to maximize government incentives. We utilized the government's PACE loan, a program designed to encourage energy-efficient and renewable energy projects. For projects like this, the PACE loan can forgive a significant portion of the investment. In this Texas energy community, 40% of a $100 million loan was forgivable, dramatically reducing the financial burden and enhancing the project's viability.

The financial structure of a Grande Solar Farm is significantly bolstered by a combination of tax incentives and forgivable loans. These include a 30% Investment Tax Credit, a 21% benefit from accelerated depreciation, and an additional 10% tax credit for employing domestic products—though it's worth noting that the specifics of this are under IRS review. Moreover, building within an energy community adds another 10% tax credit. When you account for the 40% forgivable portion of the PACE loan for projects in specific zip codes, the return on investment becomes extraordinarily attractive, potentially reaching an ROI of 111%.

In Texas, the financial returns from a solar farm can vary significantly based on the method used to sell electricity. Typically, selling electricity back to the grid might offer a rate of about 3.7 cents per kilowatt-hour (kWh). However, there's a more lucrative route: selling directly to retail clients. By choosing this path, investors can significantly increase their earnings, potentially receiving 15 cents/kWh, while the marketing agency responsible for selling the power purchase agreements (PPAs) might earn 5 cents/kWh. The retail clients would be charged around 20 cents per kWh, offering them a competitive rate compared to the 22.5 cents per kWh they would typically pay to the grid. This direct-to-consumer approach enhances the profit potential for the solar farm's investors by bypassing the grid's lower payment rates.

As we look forward to 2024, there's promising news on the horizon for those interested in investing in renewable energy projects like solar farms. While the last round of PACE Loans closed on September 30, 2023, the government's track record of supporting renewable energy initiatives suggests new programs, similar to PACE or other forgivable loan programs, should reopen again very soon for 2024. These programs have historically provided substantial financial incentives to encourage the development of energy-efficient and renewable energy projects. Moreover, grant programs that offer hundreds of millions of dollars for Decarbonization will emerge as particularly beneficial for solar farms. These grants can offer additional financial support to make solar projects even more viable and attractive.

The constant evolution of government incentives and financial aid programs underscores the importance of staying informed and ready to capitalize on these opportunities as they arise. By understanding and leveraging these incentives, investors can significantly enhance the profitability and feasibility of their solar farm projects. The case of the Texas Solar Farm in an energy community illustrates just how transformative these incentives can be—turning substantial investments into highly profitable and environmentally friendly enterprises.

To ensure you don't miss out on any upcoming programs or incentives that could benefit your solar energy investments, follow me on LinkedIn and subscribe to my newsletter Linkedin Newsletters.

https://www.linkedin.com/in/sharkdavidvogel/

Staying informed with the latest and most accurate information will enable you to make timely, strategic decisions in the renewable energy market. As government programs continue to evolve, being proactive and well-informed will be key to maximizing the return on your investment in the renewable energy sector.

The True Treasure

With a solar farm valued at $100 million, primarily underwritten by government incentives like forgivable loans, the true treasure unfolds in the 25-year odyssey of electricity generation that ensues. Once operational, the solar farm morphs into a ceaseless revenue-churning behemoth. The electricity harvested holds the promise to retail at a sum exceeding $40 million annually, embodying a veritable treasure chest of earnings under the radiant Texan sun.

It's crucial to underscore that the $40 million benchmark is a gross revenue estimate, realized only if you channel electricity directly to retail consumers as opposed to the grid. The narrative of net revenue ascends to a substantially more lucrative plateau, particularly when the electricity is sold at retail, unveiling a financial panorama ripe with potential and profitability in the heart of Texas.

The Texan market, known for its liberal energy market, provides the flexibility to sell electricity directly to retail clients, bypassing the grid's constraints. This flexibility is a significant tide in favor of solar investments. When you delve into the numbers, the narrative becomes even more compelling.

The essence of this venture is both in immediate returns and the long-term value generated over 25 years of electricity production. The government incentives, including forgivable loans, form the sails that propel the solar farm venture into a horizon of continual revenue generation. Texas, with its energy-free market, is the wind that promises a smooth sail through the waves of electricity retail, ensuring that the solar farm isn't just a one-time investment, but a legacy of renewable prosperity.

CHAPTER 13

A Solar Secret Too Powerful To Keep Hidden

The vast expanse of the business world is like an unending ocean, replete with timeless wisdom and guarded secrets; among them is the often-heard advice to never reveal your 'secret sauce'. Yet, as I delved deeper into the expansive and intricate solar industry, I encountered a profound epiphany. Not all secrets need to be zealously guarded like sunken treasure. Indeed, some are meant to be shared, especially when they hold the power to illuminate paths and empower others.

With the boldness characteristic of a shark navigating through the deep blue, I decided to shed light on one particularly luminous secret: the art of securing a $100 Million PACE Loan from the Government to construct a solar farm, with an astonishing 40% of that amount forgivable.

> **Note:** Pace Loans are 20% to 60% forgivable, but in this case study, an Energy Community in Texas, the forgivable portion is 40%.

This revelation was not met without its share of consternation. Recently, a look of unmistakable dismay crossed the face of one of my trusted sales representatives. The cause of her unease? My decision to unveil this potent secret was a move she deemed too audacious.

But why keep such powerful knowledge under wraps when it can lead to monumental strides in sustainable development?

Orchestrating a colossal $100 million *Grande Solar Farm* construction, heavily underwritten by government incentives through forgivable loans and assorted tax credits, isn't just an investment; it's the closest thing to a sure thing I have ever seen on Wall Street.

The real allure, however, isn't just in the financial figures but in mastering the intricate dance with government financing—a dance that many perceive as a cryptic, almost labyrinthine, endeavor.

The journey to uncovering and utilizing these government funds is complex and layered, much like deciphering an ancient, arcane text. It requires patience, persistence, and a deep understanding of legislative nuances. It's about aligning one's investment vision with the shifting sands of government policies and incentives, navigating through the bureaucratic tapestry with a mix of finesse and boldness. In sharing this 'secret sauce', my aim isn't just to boast about a successful strategy but to pave the way for more to join in this lucrative yet noble venture of harnessing the sun's power.

This is the thrilling reality of the solar sector: a realm where audacity meets opportunity, where the secrets of yesterday become the guiding beacons of tomorrow. It's a testament to the fact that in the right hands, knowledge isn't just power—it's a catalyst for innovation and a cornerstone for building a brighter, greener future. So, with the spirit of a pioneer and the strategic acumen of a seasoned entrepreneur, I say to you; Dive into these waters, to understand, utilize, and perhaps even expand upon this revealed secret, as we collectively strive towards a more sustainable and prosperous horizon.

By offering billionaires and centi-millionaires knowledge they weren't privy to, I'm laying down a feast of opportunities. This approach, inspired by the wisdom of Jay Abraham, a marketing and business genius, revolves around the principle of giving generously upfront.

Fellow voyagers, as we navigate these waters, let's remember: being transparent, and being generous with knowledge might seem counterintuitive in the short run (at least to some of my sales reps), but in the vast ocean of business, it's the strategic, unexpected moves that often lead to the most exhilarating, rewarding adventures.

In this journey of revelation and grand ventures, the endpoint is just as pivotal as the beginning. As we near the close of this chapter, let's consider the horizon beyond the solar farm's last panel and the final cent of investment returned. The legacy we're creating isn't measured in megawatts alone but in the ripples of change, we catalyze across communities and industries. By demystifying the grandeur of government-backed solar investments, we're not just erecting solar panels; we're constructing beacons of hope and progress.

This path, illuminated by the shared secret of leveraging substantial PACE Loans and other government incentives, is more than a route to financial success. It's a testament to the transformative power of shared knowledge and collective ambition. As more investors and entrepreneurs are emboldened by this insight, the landscape of renewable energy will expand, bringing us closer to a future where sustainable power is not the exception but the norm.

So, to the trailblazers, the dreamers, and the relentless seekers of the next big leap: the journey doesn't end here. It's an ongoing saga of growth, learning, and legacy-building. As the sun rises on new opportunities and sets on outdated practices, let's embrace the warmth of knowledge shared and the brilliance of a future forged together. Let's continue to dive deep, push boundaries, and invest not just in solar farms but in the very fabric of our future.

In sharing this powerful secret, we've unlocked more than just financial gains; we've opened the door to a community of forward-thinkers and change-makers. This isn't just about one solar farm or one investment;

it's about setting a precedent for what can be achieved when we unite under the banner of innovation and sustainability. As the tides of business ebb and flow, let's ride the waves with courage, generosity, and an unwavering commitment to a brighter, greener world. The secret's out, and the future's ours to shape. Join me in this quest, and together, let's turn the whisper of today's solar secret into tomorrow's roar of triumph.

The Best Shark Investment?

It's not in stocks, real estate, or gold. It's to build a solar farm. Let's break it down using a simple calculator. Imagine building a 100-megawatt solar farm for $100 million. With Joe Biden's Inflation Reduction Act, if you're building in an energy community, the government can give you a loan and 40% of that loan is forgivable. The words forgivable loan sound oxymoronic, but just watch the numbers. So, your cost is now down to $60 million. Now, because you're in an energy community, you receive three tax credits totaling 50%. In this scenario, that's $50 million off. You subtract that and you're down to just $10 million. You also benefit from a 21% accelerated depreciation. That leaves you at a *negative* $11 million. That's right, the government's Return On Investment (ROI) for you is a whopping 111%. But wait, it gets better. Here is where a real shark will make this investment shine. Based on our scientific algorithms, your farm will churn out an estimated $11,884,400 annually, selling electricity to the grid at 3.7 cents per kilowatt-hour.

But, I am a shark.

Why would I have my client sell to the grid for 3.7 cents when they charge the retail consumer 22 cents per kilowatt hour?

Joint venture with me or another business development expert that will market your PPA, and we'll retail that same electricity directly to consumers. After paying a reasonable commission of say five cents a kilowatt hour, as an investor, you're looking at grossing a whopping $48,180,000. Every Single Year

And with the life of the farm being 25 years or more, well, you do the math my fellow apex predators of the business world. These numbers represent an illustration, actual results may vary. But, this Shark (like Taylor Mason) is very anal about numbers and these numbers represent a very real scenario.

CHAPTER 14

Risks of Solar Investing

The journey into solar investing is an exhilarating venture into harnessing one of nature's most potent forces: the sun. This celestial body, a seemingly infinite energy sphere, bathes our planet in light and warmth, driving the very systems of life on Earth. Its power is the linchpin of solar energy investments, offering a clean, inexhaustible resource that promises to reshape our energy landscape. As we bask in the potential of solar energy, it's crucial to recognize that this endeavor, while promising, is not without its inherent risks. These risks, often dictated by the very nature of the sun and the environment it influences, form a critical part of any investor's calculus.

Firstly, the sun, for all its constancy, does not shine with uniform intensity or predictability across the globe. Solar investments hinge on the availability and consistency of sunlight, which can vary dramatically due to geographical location, season, and weather patterns. Areas prone to significant cloud cover, shorter daylight hours, or higher latitudes may experience reduced solar irradiance, directly impacting the efficiency and output of solar panels. This variability is a fundamental risk, as it can lead to fluctuations in energy production and, consequently, the financial returns of a solar project. Investors need to consider these patterns and incorporate them into their site selection, design, and financial projections to mitigate the risks associated with variable sunlight.

Beyond the daily and seasonal variations of solar exposure, solar investments are also susceptible to Acts of God—extraordinary natural events that can disrupt or even devastate solar operations. These include hurricanes, tornadoes, earthquakes, and severe hailstorms, all of which can cause catastrophic damage to solar panels and supporting infrastructure. The physical destruction brought about by such events can lead to substantial repair or replacement costs and significant operational downtime, affecting both the immediate revenue and the long-term viability of the investment. While the probability of experiencing such an event may be low in certain areas, their potential impact is so substantial that they must be factored into any comprehensive risk assessment.

The impact of climate change introduces another layer of complexity and uncertainty. As weather patterns become more extreme and unpredictable, solar investments may face new and evolving risks. Increased incidences of severe weather events, changing precipitation patterns, and shifting temperature baselines can all influence solar energy production and the physical integrity of solar installations. Investors must stay informed about the latest climate models and predictions, adjusting their risk mitigation strategies accordingly to ensure the resilience and adaptability of their solar projects.

However, it's not only the natural elements that pose risks to solar investments; the regulatory and market environments are equally critical. Changes in government policies, regulations, or subsidies can significantly affect the economic attractiveness of solar projects. Shifts in energy demand, technological advancements, or movements in the cost of alternative energy sources can all influence the market dynamics and, consequently, the success of a solar investment. Navigating these risks requires a keen understanding of the legal, political, and market landscapes, as well as the ability to adapt strategies as these external conditions evolve.

Despite these challenges, the strategic management of risks can lead to a thriving solar investment. This involves meticulous site selection, considering not just the average sunlight but also the range of potential environmental impacts. It includes investing in high-quality, durable solar equipment capable of withstanding local weather conditions and integrating advanced technologies to maximize efficiency and resilience. It requires comprehensive insurance coverage, designed to protect against a range of natural and man-made risks. It involves a flexible, informed approach to managing regulatory and market risks, staying abreast of changes, and positioning the investment to adapt and capitalize on new opportunities.

In the following sections, we will delve into each of these risk categories in more detail, providing a comprehensive overview of the challenges and strategies associated with solar investing. From understanding the technicalities of solar irradiance to navigating the complexities of climate change and regulatory environments, we'll explore the multifaceted nature of risk in this dynamic field. By the end, you'll have a deeper understanding of the risks at play and the tools and strategies at your disposal to manage them effectively.

As we embark on this detailed exploration, remember that risk, while inherent to any investment, also brings opportunities for innovation, differentiation, and competitive advantage. With the right approach, the risks associated with solar investing can be not just managed but harnessed, leading to a robust, resilient, and profitable venture into the bright future of renewable energy.

Assessing the risks involved in solar investing is critical for investors looking to venture into this growing sector. Solar energy investments, like any other investment, come with a set of risks that can impact their viability and returns. Understanding these risks is essential for making informed decisions and for the successful management of a solar investment portfolio.

General And Usual Risk Factors

1. **Market and Price Volatility:** The solar industry is subject to market fluctuations and price volatility, which can be influenced by various factors including technological advancements, changes in supply and demand, and global economic conditions. For instance, a surplus in the production of solar panels may lead to a drop in prices, affecting the profitability of solar manufacturing companies. Similarly, economic downturns can reduce investment in renewable energy projects.

2. **Technological Risks:** The solar energy sector is rapidly evolving, with continuous advancements in technology. This rapid pace of innovation can render existing solar technologies obsolete, potentially diminishing the value of previous investments. For example, newer, more efficient solar panel models can decrease the competitiveness of older installations.

3. **Regulatory and Policy Risks:** Government policies and regulations play a significant role in the solar energy sector. Changes in government incentives, subsidies, and regulatory frameworks can significantly impact the solar market. For instance, the reduction or elimination of tax credits and subsidies can increase the cost of solar projects, making them less attractive to investors.

4. **Environmental and Climatic Factors:** The performance of solar energy systems is heavily dependent on climatic conditions. Regions with less sunlight or prolonged periods of inclement weather can experience reduced solar energy output, affecting the efficiency and financial returns of solar projects. Additionally, solar installations can be susceptible to environmental risks such as natural disasters, which can cause damage to the infrastructure.

5. **Operational Risks:** Solar energy projects involve operational risks, including system performance issues, maintenance requirements, and technological faults. The efficiency of solar panels can decrease over time, and unexpected equipment failures can lead to additional costs and downtime.

6. **Financial Risks:** The initial capital expenditure for solar projects can be substantial. This high upfront cost can pose a financial risk, particularly if the expected returns on investment are not realized as planned. Fluctuating interest rates and the availability of financing options also add to the financial risk.

7. **Intermittency and Storage Challenges**: Solar energy is intermittent – it is only produced when the sun is shining. This intermittency requires effective energy storage solutions to ensure a

consistent energy supply, which can add to the complexity and cost of solar projects.

8. **Contractual and Counterparty Risks:** Solar investments often involve long-term contracts with various parties, including suppliers, contractors, and off-takers. The financial stability and performance of these counterparties can pose risks. For instance, the default of a key contractor or off-taker can jeopardize the project.

9. **Land Use and Environmental Concerns**: Large-scale solar installations require significant land, which can lead to land use conflicts and environmental concerns. The impact on local ecosystems and the potential opposition from local communities can pose risks to solar projects. Theft and Vandalism: Solar installations, often located in remote or accessible areas, are susceptible to theft and vandalism. The valuable materials in solar panels and associated equipment can attract thieves, while vandalism can cause costly damages and operational disruptions.

10. **Embezzlement and Fraud:** As with any business venture, there's a risk of embezzlement or fraud by internal staff or external contractors. This can include the misappropriation of funds, overcharging for services, or underdelivering on contractual obligations, which can significantly impact the financial health and reputation of the project.

11. **Dependency on Subsidies and Incentives:** Solar investments often rely heavily on government subsidies and incentives to be financially viable. Changes or expiration of these incentives can drastically alter the economic landscape, increasing the cost of projects or reducing their profitability.

12. **Weather-Related Damages Beyond Typical Climate Concerns:** Beyond general environmental and climatic factors, solar installations are at risk from unexpected and severe weather events such as lightning strikes, hailstorms, or prolonged periods of extreme temperatures, which can damage equipment or reduce efficiency.

13. **Cybersecurity Threats:** As solar energy systems become more integrated with smart grids and digital monitoring technologies, they become vulnerable to cybersecurity threats. Hackers could potentially disrupt operations, steal data, or even cause physical damage through remote access to system controls.

14. **Supply Chain Risks:** The manufacturing and deployment of solar panels and other components depend on complex global supply chains. Disruptions such as trade disputes, tariffs, or shortages of critical materials can lead to delays, increased costs, or availability issues, impacting the overall project timeline and cost.

15. **Land Rights and Acquisition Risks:** Securing land for solar farms can be fraught with challenges, including disputes over land rights, zoning laws, or resistance from local communities. Issues with land acquisition can delay projects, increase costs, or even render a site unusable for solar development.

16. **Connection and Grid Integration Risks:** Connecting a solar farm to the power grid involves technical, regulatory, and physical challenges. Grid instability, capacity limitations, or regulatory changes can affect the ability to efficiently and reliably feed solar-generated electricity into the grid.

17. **Obsolescence Risk due to Technological Advancements:** While technological advancements are generally positive, they can render existing solar installations obsolete or less efficient. Rapid improvements in solar technology might necessitate additional investments to upgrade or replace older systems to maintain competitiveness and efficiency.

18. **Insurance and Liability Risks:** Solar projects must be adequately insured against a range of potential issues, including accidents, natural disasters, and equipment failure. Finding and maintaining the right insurance coverage can be complex and costly, and unexpected gaps or disputes can lead to significant liabilities.

In summary, assessing the risks involved in solar investing requires a thorough understanding of the market dynamics, technological developments, regulatory environment, environmental factors, operational efficiencies, financial implications, intermittency challenges, contractual agreements, and potential land use issues. Investors must carefully consider these risks in conjunction with the potential rewards to make informed investment decisions in the solar energy sector.

CHAPTER 15

Mitigating Risk

Mitigating risks in solar investing is a multifaceted strategy that involves understanding the various challenges and systematically addressing them to reduce exposure and enhance the investment's success potential. Each point of risk identified earlier has its own set of mitigation strategies.

As we prepare to navigate the multifaceted landscape of solar investing, it is crucial to equip ourselves with a robust array of strategies to mitigate the inherent risks. What follows is a comprehensive 15-point list, each a beacon guiding us through the potential pitfalls and enhancing the resilience of our solar ventures. These strategies are not merely defensive measures but proactive steps toward securing a brighter, more sustainable future in solar energy investment. As you delve into each point, consider them as integral components of a larger blueprint designed to fortify your investment against the unpredictable yet navigable world of solar energy;

1. **Diversification:** To mitigate the impact of market and price volatility, investors can diversify their solar portfolio across different technologies, geographic locations, and market segments. This

approach spreads the risk and ensures that the adverse effect on one project does not jeopardize the entire investment portfolio. Diversification might also involve investing in different stages of solar projects or spreading investments over various solar-related industries such as manufacturing, installation, and maintenance.

2. **Staying Informed:** Keeping up-to-date with technological advancements, regulatory changes, and economic trends is vital. Regularly attending industry conferences, subscribing to reputable journals, and maintaining a network of industry contacts can provide early warnings and insights into emerging risks and opportunities. Being informed also means continuously monitoring the performance of existing investments to detect and address issues promptly.

3. **Insurance and Warranties:** Adequate insurance coverage is crucial. This includes property insurance, liability insurance, and in some cases, business interruption insurance. Manufacturers' warranties can also protect against early failures or underperformance of solar equipment. It's important to understand the specifics of insurance and warranty agreements to ensure they cover the relevant risks without significant exclusions.

4. **Partnerships and Expert Consultation:** Collaborating with experienced partners can significantly mitigate risks. This might involve

working with established solar developers, contractors, and consultants who have a proven track record. These partners can provide valuable insights into site selection, technology choices, and operational management. Legal and financial experts can guide regulatory compliance, contract structuring, and risk assessment.

5. **Long-Term Perspective:** Viewing investments from a long-term perspective is particularly important in the solar industry, where technological and regulatory landscapes are constantly evolving. This approach involves being prepared for policy shifts, price changes, and technological advancements. It also means designing and constructing solar installations with future upgrades and changes in mind.

6. **Professional Assistance for Government Incentives:** Engaging professionals who specialize in securing government incentives can enhance the financial viability of solar projects. These experts understand the intricacies of application processes for grants, loans, and tax benefits. They can navigate the bureaucratic hurdles and ensure that all possible incentives are utilized effectively.

7. **Asset Protection for Loan Liability:** When dealing with large forgivable loans, personal liability can be a significant concern. Consulting with an asset protection attorney can help structure personal and business assets to minimize exposure. This

might involve setting up trusts, creating limited liability entities, or other legal structures to protect personal assets in the event the loan forgiveness does not materialize or other liabilities arise.

8. **Weather and Environmental Adaptation:** Implementing weather-resistant designs and choosing appropriate locations can reduce the impact of environmental and climatic factors. This includes using durable materials, incorporating flexible designs that can withstand various weather conditions, and selecting sites less prone to natural disasters. Monitoring systems can also provide early warnings to minimize damage.

9. **Technological Flexibility:** Staying flexible with technology choices can mitigate the risk of obsolescence. This involves selecting modular or upgradeable systems, keeping abreast of new technologies, and being prepared to incorporate new advancements into existing installations. Regular maintenance and performance monitoring can also extend the lifespan and efficiency of solar technologies.

10. **Robust Contractual Agreements:** Detailed and robust contracts with all parties involved can provide a legal framework to address any defaults or disputes. This includes clear terms and conditions, performance guarantees, and dispute-resolution mechanisms. Contracts should be

reviewed by legal professionals to ensure they are comprehensive and enforceable.

11. **Supply Chain Management:** Developing strong relationships with suppliers and having multiple sources for critical components can mitigate supply chain risks. Understanding the entire supply chain, from raw materials to final installation, allows for better planning and response to disruptions.

12. **Regulatory Engagement:** Staying engaged with regulatory developments and participating in policy discussions can provide early insights into potential changes. It can also offer opportunities to influence policy in ways that favor solar investments.

13. **Site Security Measures:** Implementing robust security measures can protect against theft and vandalism. This might include physical barriers, surveillance systems, security patrols, and rapid response plans. Engaging with local communities can also reduce the risk of vandalism and theft.

14. **Cybersecurity Protocols:** As solar systems become more connected, implementing strong cybersecurity measures is essential. This involves regular security audits, updating systems, training staff on security practices, and having a response plan in place for any breaches.

15. **Legal and Financial Structuring:** Proper legal and financial structuring of solar projects can provide a

shield against various risks. This might involve creating special-purpose vehicles for individual projects, leveraging non-recourse financing, or engaging in risk-sharing arrangements with partners.

In conclusion, while the risks associated with solar investing are significant, they can be managed and mitigated with a comprehensive and proactive approach. This involves a combination of diversification, informed decision-making, insurance and warranties, partnerships, and a long-term perspective. By carefully addressing each risk area with targeted strategies, investors can navigate the complexities of the solar market and enjoy the substantial rewards that solar investments can offer.

CHAPTER 16

$35 Million Grants for Mega Polluters

As we approach the dawn of 2024, I am thrilled to share with you a pivotal opportunity that lies on the horizon for the industrial and energy sectors. My prediction for the coming year centers on the resurgence of Decarbonization Grants – a transformative initiative that is set to redefine the landscape of industrial operations.

Last year, these grants, ranging impressively from $35 million to $500 million (EACH!), played a crucial role in incentivizing businesses to pivot towards more sustainable practices. It's important to note that these grants are dynamic; they open and close, and their details are subject to evolution. Staying abreast of these changes will be key to capitalizing on these opportunities.

Getting Paid To Be A Good Corporate Citizen

Let me share with you a somewhat humorous tale that I recently recounted to a client. Picture President Joe Biden, armed with a colossal checkbook, standing at the gates of these mega-polluters. In a twist of fate, he's not there to chastise but to incentivize. *"Here's a boatload of cash,"* he says, *"Stop being the environment's nemesis; become its hero instead."*

It's a narrative that, while injected with humor, underscores a critical message: The administration is willing to invest heavily in those willing to pivot toward sustainable practices.

In 2024, I will be focusing on helping clients streamline these large Decarbonization Grants as they open. These aren't your average grants, as we're talking about major-league funding earmarked for the transformation of the most significant carbon-emitting factories. These facilities, long regarded as the arch-villains of environmental degradation, now have a chance to redeem themselves. It's an opportunity for the *"worst of the worst"* offenders to make a turnaround that could redefine their legacy.

This scenario is a clarion call to owners and operators of these industrial behemoths. The Decarbonization Grants of 2024 will not just be an infusion of funds; they are a lifeline to pivot your operations toward a sustainable future. By availing these grants, not only do you align with global environmental standards, but you also reposition your company at the forefront of the green industrial revolution.

Most importantly, it's about putting green in your wallet – Joe Biden is essentially paying you to be moral!

As we step into 2024, let us embrace the challenge and opportunity to be architects of change. Together, we can steer our enterprises towards a future that is not only profitable but also sustainable and ethical.

CHAPTER 17

THE POLITICAL FUTURE OF SOLAR

Welcome to the fascinating realm of American politics, where the game isn't always chess; it can resemble a round of musical chairs. Right in the center of this political whirlwind, where ideologies shift like dunes, we find a radiant protagonist - solar power. Today, let's dissect the intriguing confluence of politics and solar power, as orchestrated by the Inflation Reduction Act.

But first, a quick primer. In the theater of economics, 'corporate welfare' is a star performer. In simple terms, it refers to government subsidies, grants, or favorable tax treatments bestowed upon corporations and/or favored industries. Some critics argue it's a murky pool where public money is handed over to private coffers. Yet, it remains a powerful tool for the government to encourage particular industries, innovations, or practices.

In the current Democratic era, a veritable solar bonanza has been unlocked by the Inflation Reduction Act. The Act, in its magnanimous gesture, ensures that even the smallest of rural enterprises can relish a staggering 111% to 121% in federal grants and rebates on solar energy investments ranging from

$50,000 to $2 million. For the urban goliaths, a jaw-dropping grant of $35 million to a colossal half billion dollars beckons, provided they pledge allegiance to the solar cause.

Indeed! A CEO who strategically navigates the green energy wave could find their corporation a recipient of an astounding $500 million grant! With some guidance from a GPA Member, this could very well be your reality.

In any event in business, it is all about money. One fiercely Republican client of mine confessed, *"I hate Joe Biden, but I sure don't mind cashing his checks!"* Now that's an admission you won't find on Fox News!

That said, politics is fickle. While Democrats have steered the ship towards a sunnier horizon, a right shift in political winds could potentially bring in storm clouds. Today's beneficiaries could be tomorrow's has-beens.

But hold on, there's a twist in the tale. Cue, Governor Ron DeSantis of Florida - the likely GOP Presidential nominee. A surprising sun worshiper amidst his party ranks, DeSantis's solar leanings have even caught the eye of solar visionary Elon Musk. Could this herald a greener shift within the GOP, traditionally seen as oil loyalists?

Political tides might turn, but corporate welfare remains a constant undercurrent. The GOP and Democrats have their pet projects and favored industries. Billions are disbursed like a magician's deck of cards - the recipients just vary with the ruling party.

Amidst this reality, our plea is simple: Let solar energy rise above partisan politics. With its potential to create jobs, boost the economy, and protect our planet, it's high time this issue basks in bipartisan support.

As we navigate this political labyrinth, let's remember to seize the sunny opportunities today's administration offers while advocating for a future where solar energy is universally championed - irrespective of who resides in the White House.

To conclude, no matter who triumphs in the political arena - be it Biden or DeSantis - let's ensure that the real victor is solar power. Because ultimately, the sun doesn't care about party lines, and neither should our energy policy.

CHAPTER 18

MAKING YOUR MOVE

The question that remains is how you, as an individual investor, can capitalize on this burgeoning field and make a shark-sized investment play. Your path in solar investing is largely determined by your financial standing. This book has laid the groundwork, and now it's time to tailor this knowledge to fit your specific situation. Here, we categorize potential investors into three distinct groups, each with its unique strategy for solar investment:

Non-Accredited Investors:

If your net worth is less than $1 million and you are not an accredited investor, direct investment in certain funds might be off-limits. However, that doesn't mean the doors to the solar industry are closed to you. Ambition and resourcefulness can carve out a niche even here. One lucrative way is to refer Projects like REAP deals, to my firm or one like that. By identifying potential projects and referring them to the right entities, you can earn a "*shark-sized*" royalty, making a significant entry into the solar space without direct investment. This path is about leveraging your knowledge and network to facilitate solar investments.

Millionaire to Decamillionaire—Accredited Investors:

As a member of this category, you're positioned to take more substantial actions. Your journey involves assembling a team or partnering with a firm that can navigate the complexities of solar investment. This includes finding a proficient grant writer to tap into the myriad of available solar grants, a product procurement specialist to ensure you're investing in efficient and durable technology, and an installation manager to oversee the implementation of solar projects. My firm offers these services, and while I might be biased, as a "shark" in the industry, our expertise and comprehensive approach speak for themselves. For you, the goal is to strategically invest in solar projects or companies, leveraging professional expertise to maximize returns.

Centi-millionaires and Above—High Net Worth Investors:

For those in the highest echelon of financial resources, solar investing opens up a realm of substantial opportunities. Your focus might shift towards larger-scale investments, such as funding entire solar farms, initiating community solar programs, or even venturing into innovative solar technologies. The scale of investment and potential returns are significant, with opportunities to not only increase your net worth but also to lead in the global transition to renewable energy. Your investments can shape industries, influence policies, and leave a lasting impact on the global energy landscape.

This book has explored in detail a clear roadmap to harness the sun's power effectively and profitably, regardless of your current financial standing. The sun shines for everyone, and so does the opportunity for solar investing. Your journey in solar begins now, with the decisions you make and the actions you take.

The call to action isn't just about making a move; it's about making a significant, shark-sized splash in the vast ocean of solar investing. With 23 million millionaires in the USA alone and the transformative Rural Energy for America Program (REAP) grants at your disposal, the stage is set for a monumental shift. The opportunity to invest and make a substantial impact is knocking, and it's time to open the door wide.

The Golden Opportunity with REAP

Imagine the impact if just a fraction of the 23 million millionaires in the USA directed their resources toward solar energy. The REAP is a beacon of hope, offering a substantial incentive for those ready to invest in rural America's green future. The government is essentially extending a gift, an invitation to propel the nation toward sustainability. If you're not in a rural area, it's time to network, find a partner who is, and tap into this lucrative opportunity. Investing in a Green Fund, including the one I am spearheading, opens up a realm of possibilities. These funds are designed to pool resources and invest in scalable, impactful solar projects, offering a unique blend of ethical and financial returns.

The Exclusive Club Of Centi-Millionaires

For the 28,420 centi-millionaires, you stand in a class of your own. Rare, yes, but not unique, and certainly in the position to make waves.

The term "*picking up another unit*" in your lexicon signifies acquiring another hundred million dollars, a feat that's not just a dream but a distinct possibility with the right moves in solar investing. The key is not to hesitate but to pounce.

Consider the case of the PACE loan in Texas, which offered a staggering 40% forgiveness for building a solar farm. Opportunities like these are golden, but they don't wait around. They closed swiftly, and those who hesitated missed out. As a centi-millionaire, your strategy should be to be ever-ready, and ever-vigilant for the next big opportunity. When the window opens again in 2024, be prepared to leap. With $40 million potentially forgivable, the stakes are high, and the rewards are higher.

A Call to Action That Resonates

The time for contemplation is over. The time for action is now. The solar investing landscape is ripe with opportunity, but it requires decisive, swift action. Whether you're an aspiring investor with less than a million to your name or a seasoned centi-millionaire, the path is laid out for you. For the non-accredited, leverage your networks, refer projects, and earn royalties. For millionaires to decamillionaires, assemble your team, find the grants, and strategically invest in projects or companies. And for the centi-millionaires, lead the charge in large-scale investments, shape industries, and leave a legacy.

Join the Movement, Illuminate the World

As you stand at this pivotal moment, remember that every green initiative counts. The journey of a thousand miles begins with a single step, and your first step is to seize the solar opportunity.

This isn't just an investment in solar energy; it's an investment in the future of our planet. It's a commitment to a cleaner, healthier world for generations to come. As you embark on this journey, remember that with great resources comes great responsibility. The sun's energy is limitless, and so is the potential for change. So, make your move, be a beacon of change, and together, let's illuminate the world.

With every decision you make, and every action you take, you're not just investing in solar; you're becoming a part of a larger movement, a collective force driving towards a sustainable future. So, take this knowledge, this inspiration, and turn it into action. The future is waiting, and it's radiantly bright.

As this book closes, let it be the beginning of your most impactful chapter yet. The world is ready for change. Are you?

FOLLOW THE AUTHOR

David is keenly interested in engaging with readers, professionals, and fellow enthusiasts in the field of renewable energy and sustainable development. Whether you have inquiries, comments, proposals, or serious business propositions, David welcomes your communication and looks forward to the opportunity to discuss these vital topics further or explore potential collaborations.

Feel free to reach out via email at:

david@sunrize.homes

Stay connected and updated with David's latest thoughts, publications, and projects by following him on LinkedIn and subscribing to his newsletters.:

https://www.linkedin.com/in/sharkdavidvogel/

Your insights and proposals are valuable, and David appreciates your interest and support in driving forward the conversation on solar energy and sustainability. Together, let's illuminate a path towards a brighter, greener future.

ACCREDITED INVESTORS' VENTURE OPPORTUNITIES

If you are an "*accredited investor*" and would be interested in being advised about special investment venture opportunities in Green Energy we offer, please copy the page below and send it back to us.

REQUEST FOR INFORMATION ON SPECIAL INVESTMENT VENTURE OPPORTUNITIES

I certify by my signature I am an accredited investor since (a) my individual net worth exclusive of my residence or joint net worth with my spouse exceeds $1,000,000, or (b) my individual income, is in excess of $200,000, or joint income with my spouse is in excess of $300,000, for each of 2021, 2022, 2023, and reasonably expected for 2024.

I would like to receive investment information intended exclusively for accredited investors only.

Name

Address

City, State, Zip

Business Phone, Cell Phone

Email Address

Date

Type Your First and Last Name (E-Signature)

To complete this form online, Please Scan the QR-Code or visit the Link

https://forms.gle/fveeJqLaLiWArXKy6

SOLARGRANTFINDER™

In the spirit of innovation and ahead of schedule, fueled by relentless passion, we are thrilled to unveil SolarGrantFinder™ (SGF). This innovation is meticulously crafted to revolutionize your journey in green energy projects. SGF bridges the gap between aspirations and realization, offering unparalleled financial solutions in the realm of solar investments.

What exactly is SolarGrantFinder™? At its core, SolarGrantFinder™ is an AI-powered platform, marrying advanced technology with the personal touch of human expertise. Whether you're a grassroots startup or a sprawling corporation, SGF serves as your definitive guide to navigating the expansive world of grants, subsidies, and forgivable loans tailored for solar and green projects.

Who stands to benefit from SolarGrantFinder™?

The Business Maven: For businesses aiming for a green transition, SGF identifies government subsidies reaching up to 121% on solar energy system purchases. We are committed to helping you tap into every available cent to fund your environmentally-conscious endeavors.

The Solar Investor: If your focus is on lucrative investments, SGF meticulously identifies opportunities using advanced analytics. For instance, SGF helped identify a $100 million loan opportunity for a client who wanted to build a solar farm, and because of his location, the loan would be 40% forgivable. We make the math simple and your investments shine brighter.

The Solar Sales Maestro: For those on the frontline selling solar solutions, SGF is your essential companion, giving you that extra edge in every sales pitch.

Join the Movement: We believe in the potential of every environmentally-conscious project. But more than that, we believe in YOU. This is why we've brought SolarGrantFinder™ to you ahead of schedule – because the time to act for our planet is now. The Next Step? Harness the power of SolarGrantFinder™ today. Dive into the ocean of opportunities, and let's illuminate the world together. Remember, every green initiative counts, and with SGF by your side, the path to realizing those initiatives becomes clearer.

Interested in working with me and SGF? Contact me today by email or on LinkedIn.

david@sunrize.homes

https://www.linkedin.com/in/sharkdavidvogel/

Remember, SGF is a combination of advanced AI with human oversight and input. Your aspirations deserve the best, and with SGF, they meet the power of endless possibilities. So, whether you're looking to invest, sell, or simply transition to greener solutions, SolarGrantFinder™ is your key.

And for those who share our vision, be our ambassadors. Refer SolarGrantFinder™ to others in your network and let's grow this community of eco-warriors. As we progress, we're constantly looking for partnerships, collaborations, and visionaries to journey with us. So, if you're seeking a partnership or considering a business proposition, we are all ears.

For "CEOs" Of Small Towns, Schools, And Universities

Leaders of schools, towns, and rural communities! As the CEOs of your domains, you are the generals on the ground, shaping the future of education and local governance. This chapter is a clarion call to action, urging you to seize every opportunity and every dollar of federal funding available under initiatives like the Inflation Reduction Act. You have the power and responsibility to transform your institutions and communities into models of sustainability and innovation. As a public servant living in a small town, I understand the challenges and opportunities you face. Let's embark on this journey to build stronger, more resilient, and greener communities together. The Inflation Reduction Act provides substantial federal grant funding for green energy projects. Understand how your school, town, or county can benefit from investments in solar installations, electric vehicle stations, and carbon emissions reduction efforts. Learn about the significant long-term financial and environmental advantages these initiatives offer, and how they can revolutionize the way your community operates and is perceived.

A Bold Call to Educational and Municipal Leaders

Esteemed administrators, university deans, high school principals, and town leaders, as you stand at the forefront of guiding our communities and educational institutions, a groundbreaking opportunity awaits. This chapter serves as a potent call to action, a rallying cry to seize a moment that promises not only to revolutionize your fiscal landscape but also to significantly bolster the sustainability and vitality of your domains. Billions in federal grants are available to eliminate your electric bills, transform your infrastructure, and lead your communities into a new era of environmental stewardship and financial liberation.

The Billions at Your Doorstep: Understanding the Opportunity

As leaders entrusted with the future of educational excellence and community well-being, you are uniquely positioned to capitalize on an unprecedented opportunity. The Inflation Reduction Act, among other initiatives, has earmarked billions of dollars specifically for entities ready to embrace renewable energy solutions. These funds are not merely incentives; they are powerful catalysts for change, offering you the chance to radically diminish or even eliminate your institutions' and communities' electric bills while contributing to a global movement of environmental responsibility.

The Call to Eliminate Electric Bills: A Financial and Environmental Revolution

Imagine a future where your school or town no longer faces the burden of escalating electric costs. A future where renewable energy sources power your operations, freeing up funds for educational programs, community services, and infrastructure improvements. This vision is not a distant dream but a tangible reality made possible through the strategic utilization of green grants. By investing in solar panels, electric vehicle charging stations, and other green initiatives, you can dramatically reduce your energy expenses and even generate revenue, all while significantly reducing your carbon footprint.

Don't Overlook This: The Perils of Inaction

In the face of such an opportunity, inaction or hesitation is not merely a missed chance but a disservice to your institution and community. Every day that passes without tapping into these available funds is a day of unnecessary expenditures and missed opportunities for growth and improvement. As stewards of your communities and leaders in education, the responsibility lies with you to explore and harness these resources. The message is clear: the time for deliberation is over; the time for action is now.

Giving Back to the Community: A Personal Mission

My dedication to bringing this message to you is not just professional; it's deeply personal. As someone who has committed to helping kids and bettering communities, I understand the transformative power of education and community development. This chapter, this book, is my way of extending that commitment to you, the leaders who can enact significant change. By informing you of these grants and guiding you through the process of claiming them, I am contributing to a brighter future for all our children and communities.

The Ripple Effect: Beyond Electric Bills

The impact of transitioning to green energy extends far beyond the financial savings on electric bills. It's about setting a precedent for responsible and innovative leadership. It's about enhancing the educational experience by providing students with a living example of sustainability in action. And it's about fostering a community that values and works towards a healthier environment. By taking this step, you are not only leading your institution or town to a more sustainable future but also inspiring others to follow suit.

The Final Word: Seize the Moment

As this chapter comes to a close, the message is unequivocal and urgent: seize the moment. The billions in federal grants represent more than money; they signify a pathway to empowerment, sustainability, and long-term prosperity. As CEOs of your schools, universities, and towns, the decision to embrace this opportunity will be a defining moment in your leadership journey.

Let this chapter be the catalyst that propels you into action. Let the vision of a community-powered by clean, cost-effective energy drive your efforts. And let the promise of a brighter, greener future for all be the legacy that you strive to create. The resources are there, the benefits are clear, and the time to act is now. Be bold, be decisive, and lead the charge toward a sustainable revolution in your community. Together, let's turn this vision into a reality.

As a partner in your journey, I stand ready to assist, guide, and support your endeavors. Let's make this new year a starting point for a journey filled with growth, prosperity, and positive change. Here's to a future where every school, university, and town is a beacon of green energy and innovation. Here's to your leadership and the lasting impact it will have.

I am here to help any small-town or school/university government executive correct the # 1 biggest mistake someone in his/her position might make: Ignoring millions of dollars in government grants that are being offered to the local community!

Contact me: david@sunrize.homes

Indian Tribes Shine

There is a monumental shift poised to benefit Indian Tribes in the United States, propelling them into the forefront of solar energy production and sovereignty.

The Dawn of a New Era

The Energy Policy Act of 2005 laid the foundation for a seismic shift in energy procurement and consumption in the United States. It mandated that the federal government source a portion of its electricity from renewable sources, thus setting the stage for a deeper involvement of Indian Tribes in national energy affairs. Secretary Chu's prophetic statement from the Department of Energy illuminates the path ahead, promising preference for tribes and tribal majority-owned businesses in the renewable energy domain.

The Powering Affordable Clean Energy (PACE) Program

At the heart of this transition is the Powering Affordable Clean Energy (PACE) program, a groundbreaking initiative specifically designed to support Indian Tribes' transition to green energy. With a staggering 60% forgivable loan on offer, the PACE program is akin to a financial lifeline, dramatically reducing the economic barriers to solar adoption and allowing tribes to establish or expand their solar energy capabilities.

Financial Strategies and Investment Tax Credits

Beyond direct funding, Indian Tribes have the opportunity to leverage their unique position by selling investment tax credits, a strategy that can significantly enhance the profitability of solar ventures. This approach not only boosts the economic return on each project but also opens up avenues for reinvestment and further growth in renewable energy infrastructure.

Transforming Tribes into Solar Powerhouses

The enactment of the Inflation Reduction Act provides an unprecedented opportunity for Indian Tribes to evolve from passive participants to active leaders in the renewable energy sector. The Act facilitates the construction of new renewable energy sources on tribal lands, enabling tribes to sell solar electricity directly to one of their most reliable customers: the federal government. This arrangement fosters a mutually beneficial relationship, with the government actively preferring businesses owned and controlled by tribes.

Navigating the Market

The landscape of energy markets across the United States varies, with states adopting vertically integrated, retail choice, or mixed market structures. Each type presents unique challenges and opportunities for Indian Tribes. By understanding and strategically navigating these markets, tribes can maximize the benefits of their solar investments, catering to different customer bases and needs.

A Call to Action for Tribal Leaders

The time for Indian Tribes to claim their place in the sun is now. As leaders of your communities, you are called upon to embrace this golden opportunity, to harness the power of the sun, and lead your people into a future of prosperity and independence. The federal government's announcement of $7 billion in grants to empower states, municipalities, and Indian Tribes in solar advancement is not just an offer; it's an invitation to a partnership for a better future.

The Road Ahead: Illuminating America's Path Forward

Together, we stand on the brink of a new chapter in America's energy story, one where Indian Tribes play a starring role. By embracing the opportunities laid out in the Inflation Reduction Act and related programs, tribes can significantly contribute to the nation's renewable energy goals, drive economic growth, and establish a lasting legacy of environmental stewardship and cultural pride.

Conclusion

The Inflation Reduction Act is more than just legislation; it's a catalyst for change, empowering Indian Tribes to become sovereign leaders in the solar revolution. As we look to the future, the vision is clear: a nation powered by clean, sustainable energy, with Indian Tribes at the heart of this transformation. The journey to solar sovereignty is not without its challenges, but the path is illuminated with promise and potential. The time to shine is now, and the future is radiant. Indian Tribes, the future is yours to shape. Let us embark on this journey together and write a new saga of prosperity, resilience, and sustainability under the sunlit sky.

BILLIONAIRE'S TAX REDUCTION SECRET

Welcome to this SPECIAL REPORT for CEOs who preside over their businesses. The treasure trove awaiting you? A possible 90% reduction in your income tax—an attractive prospect for any business-savvy individual. Don't hesitate to share this report with your network; they'll certainly appreciate the tip!

Imagine this: the U.S. Virgin Islands, is not just a tropical paradise, but a beacon atop the mountain of global tax havens. If your income derives from a business, these islands may be the answer to lightening your tax load—a staggering 90% off your income tax, provided you meet a set of easy-to-comprehend criteria. With this, you may just find the key to your financial nirvana here on Earth.

Let's unravel the world's best-kept secret: a tax shelter paradise. The ultra-rich, spanning billionaires to deca-millionaires across the USA, are making their home amidst the sandy beaches of the U.S. Virgin Islands. The allure? A tantalizing 90% tax credit on business income, attainable through the establishment of an Economic Development Corporation.

Intrigued but skeptical?

Let's dissect the details of this 90% tax cut.

Engaging in the U.S. Virgin Islands tax shelter journey requires meeting certain requirements. These are non-negotiable and form the gateway to a 90% tax cut on your income tax from business earnings. Initially, you must establish an Economic Development Corporation for your business (akin to setting up a corporation on the mainland), and then:

- Local Employment: A fundamental requirement mandates the employment of at least ten Virgin Island natives who've resided on the islands for a minimum of one year before employment. This boosts the local economy and fortifies community bonds. Note: Branch offices can be maintained globally or throughout the USA with any number of employees worldwide.

- A minimum of 183 days must be spent annually on one of the three USVI gems—St. Croix, St. Thomas, or St. John. It's quite the hardship, indeed. Over half your year among stunning tropical landscapes, to the soothing sounds of palm trees and the serene ebb and flow of the ocean, under the gaze of a grand sky. Plus, the potential for mingling with billionaires and elite yacht clubs might just be daunting enough to deter some. But if you can brave this, the USVI provides an almost tax-free haven.

- Investment Commitment: An obligation to pledge a minimum investment of $100,000 (excluding inventory) in an enterprise that propels the Virgin Islands' economy. Your investment is the key to local economic growth.

- Understanding IRS Code: You must comprehend IRS Code sections 934 and 937. This knowledge is vital for adherence to these regulations and the subsequent enjoyment of tax benefits.

- Legal Compliance: Strict adherence to federal and local laws is crucial. Respect for and adherence to the regulations of the U.S. Virgin Islands is paramount.

- Public Beach Access: If your business is situated on the beachside, you must allow public access to your beach or shoreline. This accessibility fosters community spirit and encourages the shared enjoyment of natural beauty.

Consider Aaron, a software developer based in America's Midwest heartland. His sought-after software solutions amassed global sales of $6 million each year, equating to a corporate profit of around $2.6 million. Life was good, except for the $1.2 million annual tax bill that clouded his success.

While navigating tax laws, Aaron discovered the concept of an Economic Development Corporation

(EDC) in the USVI. The potential of reducing his yearly personal income tax bill by 90% piqued his interest. Skeptical yet captivated, he ventured further. The idea of merging his software passion with a dream life in paradise was too compelling to ignore.

So Aaron took the plunge. He moved his operations to St. Thomas, one of the USVI's shining trio. He employed ten residents, fostering a strong community bond. In his new island home, Aaron continued his software development, his workspace now graced by the calming rhythms of crashing waves. His beach location was not just a workspace but a spot where locals could enjoy the surrounding natural beauty.

A year later, Aaron's tax bill shrunk from $1.2 million to just $120,000! The savings were colossal, but the gains extended beyond money. He found a balance between work and life he'd never thought achievable, all while contributing positively to his new community. Aaron's story serves as an inspiration to entrepreneurs paying high taxes, urging them to explore the exciting opportunities of the USVI.

The 90% cut isn't just for smaller enterprises. Even larger corporations can significantly reduce their tax burden. We've seen cases where a business saved an astounding $50 million in a year, thanks to the Economic Development Corporation (EDC) and the government's liberal interpretation of "eligible business activity." Almost any non-public business can qualify with the right legal and accounting guidance.

Does it sound too easy?

Well, it is!

In summary: Set up an EDC, relocate your thriving business headquarters to the sun-drenched shores of the U.S. Virgin Islands, employ a local workforce of ten, bask in a tropical paradise for 183 days annually, and invest a minimum of $100,000. In return, you unlock an astounding array of tax benefits.

This astonishing tax relief package isn't a mirage. It's real, and it awaits you in the U.S. Virgin Islands!

One Last Note: Share this gem with a colleague feeling the tax pinch; they'll surely thank you! Stay sharp, stay curious, and swim fast. Remember, in this business ocean, if you're not the shark, you're the bait.

Earth's Expected Chill and the Alarming Warming Reality

The Earth's climate operates under a delicate balance influenced by natural cycles, which historically have led to periods of both warming and cooling. These cycles, such as the Milankovitch cycles, solar activity variations, and volcanic activity, have suggested that we might be due for a period of cooling. However, the planet is currently experiencing an alarming and counterintuitive warming trend. This paper explores the scientific underpinnings of the expected natural cooling period, how human activities have overridden this trajectory, and the grave consequences of continued global warming.

Earth's Natural Climate Cycles

The Earth's climate has undergone numerous changes throughout its history, often attributed to the Milankovitch cycles. These cycles are long-term variations in the Earth's orbit and tilt, affecting the distribution and intensity of sunlight received by the Earth, thus influencing climatic patterns. Over tens of thousands of years, these cycles have been responsible for the ice ages and warmer interglacial periods. The current phase of these cycles would suggest a gradual movement towards cooler temperatures, a trend supported by historical patterns and geological records.

Additionally, solar activity, characterized by the ebb and flow of sunspots and solar flares, impacts the amount of solar energy Earth receives. During periods known as solar minimums, reduced solar activity has historically led to cooler temperatures. Similarly, large volcanic eruptions can propel vast quantities of ash and sulfur dioxide into the stratosphere, reflecting sunlight away from the Earth and inducing short-term cooling effects, as evidenced in historical events like the "Year Without a Summer" in 1816 following the eruption of Mount Tambora.

The Anthropogenic Overdrive of Global Warming

Contrary to the natural expectation of cooling, the Earth is undergoing a rapid warming phase, the pace and scale of which are unprecedented in the context of natural variability. The primary driver of this anomalous warming is the increased concentration of greenhouse gasses in the atmosphere due to human activities. The burning of fossil fuels, deforestation, and industrial processes have elevated levels of carbon dioxide, methane, and other greenhouse gasses, enhancing the greenhouse effect and trapping more heat within the Earth's atmosphere.

The evidence for this warming is irrefutable. Global temperature records indicate a significant increase over the past century, particularly over the last few decades. The consequences of this warming are widespread and devastating. Polar ice caps and glaciers are melting at alarming rates, contributing to rising sea levels and the loss of crucial habitats. Extreme weather events such as hurricanes, heatwaves, and heavy precipitation have become more frequent and severe, causing widespread destruction and loss of life.

Current and Future Consequences of Ignoring Natural Cooling Signals

The defiance of Earth's natural cooling signals has profound implications. As the planet warms, ecosystems are pushed beyond their ability to adapt, resulting in biodiversity loss and extinction of species. Agricultural systems face unpredictability and declining yields, threatening food security for billions. Water scarcity and quality issues are exacerbated, affecting human health and leading to conflicts.

The current impacts are particularly evident in vulnerable regions. Africa, with its limited adaptive capacity, is experiencing increased droughts and famines, affecting the livelihoods and survival of millions. California's devastating wildfires, intensified by drier and hotter conditions, serve as a stark reminder of climate change's immediate effects.

The Urgent Need for Action

This alarming divergence from Earth's expected cooling path is a clarion call for immediate and decisive action. Mitigation strategies focusing on reducing greenhouse gas emissions are critical. Transitioning to renewable energy sources, enhancing energy efficiency, and protecting and restoring forests are among the key measures needed to curb the warming trend. Adaptation strategies are also crucial to reduce vulnerability and build resilience in the face of inevitable climate impacts.

International cooperation and commitment to agreements like the Paris Accord are vital to ensuring collective action. Policymakers, businesses, and individuals must all play a role in this global effort. The cost of inaction far outweighs the investments required to transition to a sustainable and resilient future.

Conclusion

The Earth's current warming trend is a stark deviation from the expected natural cooling cycle, driven predominantly by human-induced greenhouse gas emissions. The consequences of this warming are dire and wide-ranging, affecting every aspect of life on Earth. It is imperative that society acknowledges the severity of this issue and takes immediate action to mitigate and adapt to climate change. Only through concerted global efforts can we hope to realign with a sustainable path and secure a livable future for all species, including our own. As stewards of the Earth, it is our responsibility to respond to this challenge with urgency and resolve.

Tomorrow is Today For The People Of Africa Suffering From Climate Change

In 2023, the extreme weather in Africa has reached unprecedented levels, exacerbating the suffering of millions and redefining our understanding of climate change's immediacy and severity. The situation in Africa is a clarion call, urging us to reevaluate our ethical responsibilities in the face of a changing climate. The continent, known for its rich diversity, is now at the forefront of climate vulnerability.

As Neil deGrasse Tyson insightfully noted, Africa is a cradle of human diversity, home to the world's tallest, shortest, strongest, and most resilient people. Preserving this continent is crucial, not just for its inherent value but for the entire human story.

The Bible urges us to act justly and love mercy, a directive that compels us to care for our African neighbors facing the brunt of climate change.

In 2023, Africa is experiencing severe food insecurity due to climate-induced shocks, notably droughts and floods linked to the El Niño phenomenon. Countries like Ethiopia, Somalia, and Kenya are particularly affected, with 23.4 million people facing acute food insecurity. Somalia is enduring its worst hunger levels in a decade, exacerbated by the longest recorded drought in its history and catastrophic floods. This crisis highlights the increasing severity and frequency of extreme weather events globally, significantly impacting agriculture and livelihoods in vulnerable regions.

The crisis in Africa is a reflection of the broader ethical challenge posed by climate change. It confronts us with the moral imperative to act, not just as stewards of the environment, but as guardians of humanity.

Our African neighbors, bearing the brunt of climate change despite contributing least to its causes, are in dire need of this compassion and support.

In contrasting the impact of climate change between affluent regions like California and Africa, it's striking that while California faces wildfires and extreme weather, its wealth allows for recovery and resilience. In stark contrast, in Africa, particularly in countries like Ethiopia, Somalia, and Kenya, over 29 million people are grappling with relentless drought conditions. Here, the lack of resources turns these climatic phenomena into life-threatening crises, with many lives lost and millions more at risk of hunger and displacement.

This disparity underscores the uneven impact of climate change and the urgent need for a more equitable global response.

Our ethical responsibility extends beyond immediate humanitarian aid. It calls for a long-term commitment to sustainable practices, investment in renewable energy, and support for policies that mitigate the impact of climate change. This commitment is not just an environmental imperative but a moral one, deeply rooted in the principles of justice and stewardship.

As leaders, businesses, and individuals, we are called to take action, recognize the interconnectedness of our world, and work towards solutions that safeguard the future of all, especially the most vulnerable. Our actions, or inactions, will define our legacy and our humanity.

The situation in Africa is a stark reminder of the urgency of climate action. It is a call to each of us to rise to the challenge, embody the principles of ethical leadership, and ensure that our responses to climate change are as diverse and robust as the communities it affects. Let us heed this call with the seriousness it deserves, for the sake of our global community and future generations.

In conclusion, as we reflect on the plight of our African neighbors and the broader implications of climate change, let us recommit ourselves to meaningful, compassionate, and effective action.

Remember, for the people of Africa, Tomorrow is Today when it comes to climate change. Their reality of extreme weather, drought, and famine is a present crisis, not a distant threat. As global citizens and ethical leaders, it's imperative we recognize and respond to this urgency. Their struggle is a poignant reminder of our shared responsibility in combating climate change.

We should care – deeply and actively.

About The Author

David A. Vogel is a distinguished leader in the solar energy sector, serving as the CEO of White-Vogue Industries and Project SunRize. He has dedicated his career to advancing solar energy solutions and is a recognized Solar Energy Advisor known for streamlining federal grant approvals and material distribution for commercial solar projects. His expertise and innovative approaches in utilizing Artificial Intelligence and technical solutions have marked him as the founder of GEMS (Green Energy Massive Savings), helping American businesses transition to green energy and achieve substantial savings on energy costs.

As an author, lecturer, and consultant, David's extensive knowledge spans nanotechnology and AI, with a particular focus on their applications in the renewable energy sector. His strategies and insights place him at the forefront of the industry, driving growth and sustainability in businesses nationwide.

Beyond his remarkable career in solar energy, David is also a major influencer on LinkedIn, currently celebrated as a top LinkedIn Voice in Business Development. He curates three newsletters on LinkedIn that command a dedicated C-Suite following. These include a Mindful Ethics Newsletter, a Solar Commercial Investment Newsletter, and a General LinkedIn Top Followers Newsletter, each providing valuable insights and fostering discussions among industry leaders.

David's commitment to ethics and mindfulness extends into his personal life as well. He is a devout and mindful individual who passionately shares his insights through "7 at 7" — a 7-minute live sermon for Godly Mindful CEOs broadcast live on LinkedIn every morning from Sunday to Friday at 7 am. These sessions are a testament to his dedication to guiding and inspiring others toward mindful leadership and ethical business practices.

David's career is built on a foundation of diverse expertise and achievements. From starting a lucrative mail-order business in the 1970s to becoming a nationally renowned expert on rare coins and other collectibles, David has continuously evolved his professional journey. His tenure at Heritage Rare Coin

Galleries as their number-one senior numismatist and the subsequent formation of his firm underscores his entrepreneurial spirit and deep market knowledge.

David's interest extends beyond traditional financial markets into the realms of Bitcoin, electronic money, and non-fungible tokens (NFTs), reflecting his keen eye on emerging trends and technologies. His commitment to understanding and leveraging these advancements is evident in his role as a technology enthusiast with a focus on quantum physics and nanotechnology.

Beyond his professional endeavors, David is an active participant in various political, religious, and charitable organizations. He publishes newsletters that analyze economic and political trends, emphasizing the importance of informed decision-making in any financial market.

David resides in Wolfeboro, New Hampshire, and is a family man with five grown children. His interests include weightlifting, aerobics, and collecting art. Known for his love of swimming in ice-cold waters, David's unique hobbies reflect his dynamic personality and pursuit of excellence in all areas of life.

For inquiries, comments, proposals, or to discuss serious business propositions, contact David at david@sunrize.homes or text him at 802-546-1133. Join him on this journey to harness the power of the sun and drive a sustainable future for all.

Follow David Vogel on LinkedIn:

https://www.linkedin.com/in/sharkdavidvogel/

A One-Second Shark Guide to Profitable Solar Investments

Use Government Money To Fund Your Investment

A Message From David Vogel, CEO of White-Vogue Industries/Project SunRize

True leadership goes beyond guiding and mentoring; it's about giving back in tangible ways. Embodying the spirit of ethical and Mindful Godly leadership, White-Vogue Industries, under my stewardship, is proud to announce that we will be donating 3% of the profit from every commercial solar deal directly to Council For Unity to fight violence in schools. In this endeavor, we are inspired by trailblazers like Salesforce and Bombas Socks, companies that have set remarkable precedents in corporate philanthropy. Together, let's illuminate the world with both solar energy and the promise of unity and peace.

White-Vogue & Council For Unity: Green Partners Against School Violence